Jupyter Cookbook

Over 75 recipes to perform interactive computing across Python, R, Scala, Spark, JavaScript, and more

Dan Toomey

BIRMINGHAM - MUMBAI

Jupyter Cookbook

Commissioning Editor: Pravin Dhandre
Acquisition Editor: Tushar Gupta
Content Development Editor: Cheryl Dsa
Technical Editor: Sagar Sawant
Copy Editor: Vikrant Phadke, Safis Editing
Project Coordinator: Nidhi Joshi
Proofreader: Safis Editing
Indexer: Rekha Nair
Graphics: Tania Dutta
Production Coordinator: Arvindkumar Gupta

First published: April 2018

Production reference: 1270418

Published by Packt Publishing Ltd.
Livery Place
35 Livery Street
Birmingham
B3 2PB, UK.

ISBN 978-1-78883-944-0

www.packtpub.com

Mapt

Contributors

About the author

Dan Toomey has been developing applications for over 20 years. He has worked in a variety of industries and companies of all sizes, in roles ranging from sole contributor to the VP/CTO level. For the last 10 years or so, he has been contracting with companies in the eastern Massachusetts area, under Dan Toomey Software Corp. Dan has also written a few books with Packt Publishing.

About the reviewers

Nikhil Borkar holds the CQF designation and a PG degree in Quantitative Finance from the University of Mumbai. He works as an independent fintech and legal consultant. Prior to this, he was with Morgan Stanley Capital International as a Global RFP Project Manager. He has worked on Quantitative Finance and economic research projects using R, Python, and Excel VBA. He loves to approach problems in a multidisciplinary, holistic way. He is actively working on machine learning, AI, and deep learning projects.

Nikhil Akki started his career in IT support, and within a couple of years shifted to sales and marketing (after pursing MBA). Nikhil works at Deloitte in Mumbai as data science consultant. He has hands-on experience in building enterprise-grade - NLP, machine learning, and recommender system-based applications for his clients. He is often found taking up MOOCs and Kaggle problems. Prior to his current role, he taught Business Statistics at postgraduate level in an upcoming B-School in South Mumbai.

Juan Tomás Oliva Ramos is an environmental engineer from the University of Guanajuato, Mexico, with a master's degree in administrative engineering and quality. He has over five years of experience in management and development of patents, technological innovation projects, and technological solutions through statistical control of processes. He has been a teacher of statistics, entrepreneurship, and technological development since 2011. He has developed prototypes via programming and automation technologies for improvement of operations, which have been registered for patents.

I want to thank God for giving me the wisdom and humility to review this book. I thank Rubén for inviting me to collaborate on this adventure.
I want to thank my wife, Brenda, our two magic princesses (Maria Regina and Maria Renata) and Angel Tadeo), All of you are my strengths, happiness and my desire to look for the best for you.

Packt is searching for authors like you

If you're interested in becoming an author for Packt, please visit `authors.packtpub.com` and apply today. We have worked with thousands of developers and tech professionals, just like you, to help them share their insight with the global tech community. You can make a general application, apply for a specific hot topic that we are recruiting an author for, or submit your own idea.

Table of Contents

Preface

Jupyter has garnered strong interest in the data science community of late, as it makes common data processing and analysis tasks much simpler. This book is for data science professionals who want to master various tasks related to Jupyter to create efficient, easy-to-share scientific applications.

The book starts with recipes on installing and running the Jupyter Notebook system on various platforms and configuring the various packages that can be used with it. You will then see how you can implement different programming languages and frameworks on your Jupyter Notebook, such as Python, R, Julia, JavaScript, Scala, and Spark. This book contains intuitive recipes on building interactive widgets to manipulate and visualize data in real time, sharing your code, creating a multi-user environment, and organizing your Notebook. You will then get hands-on experience with JupyterLabs, microservices, and deploying them on the Web.

By the end of this book, you will have taken your knowledge of Jupyter to the next level to perform all key tasks associated with it.

Who this book is for

This cookbook is for data science professionals, developers, technical data analysts, and programmers who want to execute technical coding, visualize output, and do scientific computing with one tool. Prior understanding of data science concepts will be helpful for using this book, but it's not mandatory.

What this book covers

`Chapter 1`, *Installation and Setting up the Environment*, teaches you how to install Jupyter on different environments, such as Windows, macOS, Linux, and a server machine.

`Chapter 2`, *Adding an Engine*, shows you the steps to add these engines to your Jupyter installation so that you can script your Notebook in the language you like.

`Chapter 3`, *Accessing and Retrieving Data*, teaches how to access and retrieve data from files in different formats in Jupyter.

`Chapter 4`, *Visualize Your Analytics*, covers recipes for visualizing your analytics in Python, R, and Julia.

`Chapter 5`, *Working with Widgets*, describes the wide range of possibilities of widgets in Jupyter.

`Chapter 6`, *Jupyter Dashboards*, teaches how to install and enable Jupyter dashboards layout extension to your Notebook.

`Chapter 7`, *Sharing Your Code*, shows you several methods for sharing your Notebook with others, including using different software packages and converting the Notebook into a different form for readers without access to Jupyter.

`Chapter 8`, *Multiuser Jupyter*, explores several options for enabling Jupyter Notebooks as a multiuser platform.

`Chapter 9`, *Interacting with Big Data*, covers the methods of accessing big data from Jupyter.

`Chapter 10`, *Jupyter Security*, investigates the various security mechanisms available for your Jupyter Notebook.

`Chapter 11`, *Jupyter Labs*, lets us try new features of Jupyter in a lab environment to create our own sample Notebook.

To get the most out of this book

This book is focused on using Jupyter as a platform for data science. It assumes that you have a good understanding of data science concepts and are looking to use Jupyter as your presentation platform.

Download the example code files

You can download the example code files for this book from your account at `www.packtpub.com`. If you purchased this book elsewhere, you can visit `www.packtpub.com/support` and register to have the files emailed directly to you.

You can download the code files by following these steps:

1. Log in or register at `www.packtpub.com`.
2. Select the **SUPPORT** tab.
3. Click on **Code Downloads & Errata**.
4. Enter the name of the book in the **Search** box and follow the onscreen instructions.

Once the file is downloaded, please make sure that you unzip or extract the folder using the latest version of:

- WinRAR/7-Zip for Windows
- Zipeg/iZip/UnRarX for Mac
- 7-Zip/PeaZip for Linux

The code bundle for the book is also hosted on GitHub at `https://github.com/PacktPublishing/Jupyter-Cookbook`. If there's an update to the code, it will be updated on the existing GitHub repository.

We also have other code bundles from our rich catalog of books and videos available at `https://github.com/PacktPublishing/`. Check them out!

Download the color images

We also provide a PDF file that has color images of the screenshots/diagrams used in this book. You can download it here: `http://www.packtpub.com/sites/default/files/downloads/JupyterCookbook_ColorImages.pdf`.

Conventions used

There are a number of text conventions used throughout this book.

`CodeInText`: Indicates code words in text, database table names, folder names, filenames, file extensions, pathnames, dummy URLs, user input, and Twitter handles. Here is an example: "This script loads in `RDatasets` (this contains several standard datasets commonly used in data science)."

A block of code is set as follows:

```
Pkg.add("RDatasets")
using RDatasets
describe(dataset("datasets", "iris"))
```

When we wish to draw your attention to a particular part of a code block, the relevant lines or items are set in bold:

```
var msg = "Hello, World"
console.log(msg)
```

Any command-line input or output is written as follows:

```
python2 -m pip install ipykernel
python2 -m ipykernel install --user
```

Bold: Indicates a new term, an important word, or words that you see onscreen. For example, words in menus or dialog boxes appear in the text like this. Here is an example: "Once you select the **Install** button, Anaconda will automatically install R in your environment."

Warnings or important notes appear like this.

Tips and tricks appear like this.

Get in touch

Feedback from our readers is always welcome.

General feedback: Email `feedback@packtpub.com` and mention the book title in the subject of your message. If you have questions about any aspect of this book, please email us at `questions@packtpub.com`.

Errata: Although we have taken every care to ensure the accuracy of our content, mistakes do happen. If you have found a mistake in this book, we would be grateful if you would report this to us. Please visit `www.packtpub.com/submit-errata`, selecting your book, clicking on the Errata Submission Form link, and entering the details.

Piracy: If you come across any illegal copies of our works in any form on the Internet, we would be grateful if you would provide us with the location address or website name. Please contact us at `copyright@packtpub.com` with a link to the material.

If you are interested in becoming an author: If there is a topic that you have expertise in and you are interested in either writing or contributing to a book, please visit `authors.packtpub.com`.

Reviews

Please leave a review. Once you have read and used this book, why not leave a review on the site that you purchased it from? Potential readers can then see and use your unbiased opinion to make purchase decisions, we at Packt can understand what you think about our products, and our authors can see your feedback on their book. Thank you!

For more information about Packt, please visit `packtpub.com`.

1

Installation and Setting up the Environment

In this chapter, we will cover the following recipes:

- Installing Jupyter on Windows
- Installing Jupyter on the Mac
- Installing Jupyter on Linux
- Installing Jupyter on a server

Introduction

We will see how to install Jupyter on different environments. We will install it on Windows, the Mac, Linux, and a server machine. Some consideration should be given to multiple user access when installing on a server. If you are going to install it on a non-Windows environment, please review the Anaconda installation on Windows first as the same installation steps for Anaconda are available on other environments.

Installing Jupyter on Windows

The Windows environment suffers from a drawback: none of the standard Linux tools are available out of the box. This is a problem as Jupyter and many other programs were developed on a version of Unix and expect many developer tools normally used in Unix to be available.

Getting ready

Luckily, there is a company that has seen this problem and addressed it—Anaconda. Anaconda describes itself as a *Python Data Science Platform*, but its platform allows for a variety of solutions in data science that are not based on Python.

How to do it...

After installing Anaconda and starting Navigator, you get to a dashboard that presents the programs available, such as:

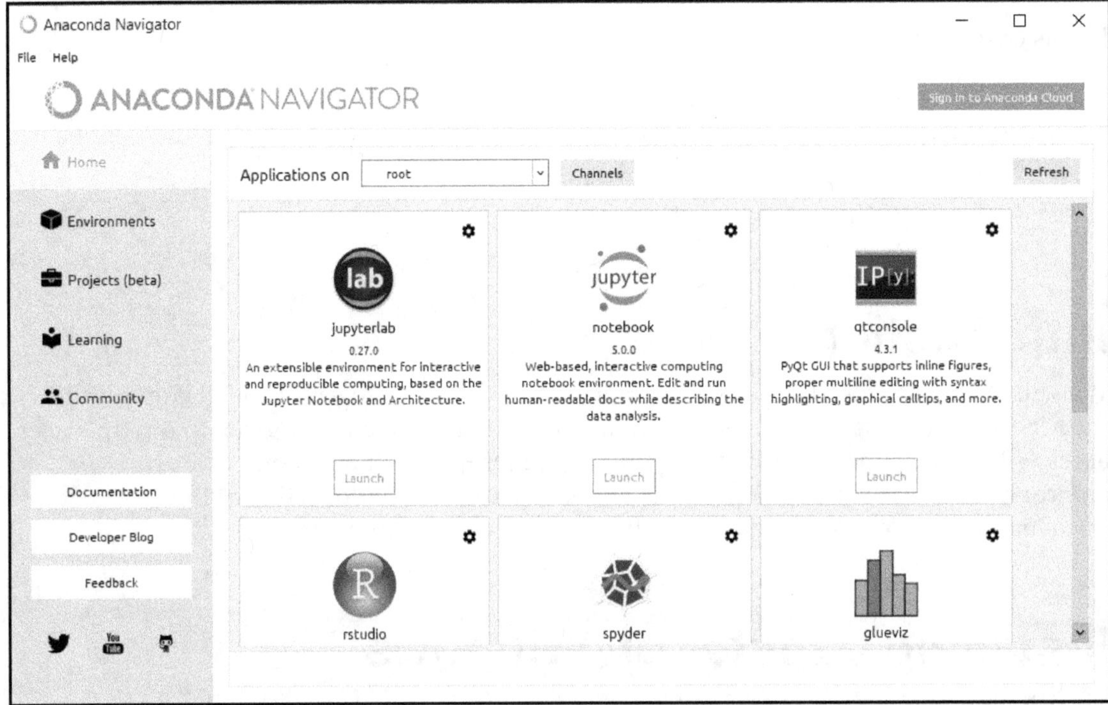

The **Anaconda Navigator** provides access to each of the programs you have installed (using Anaconda). Each of the programs can be started from Navigator (by clicking on the associated **Launch** button) and you can also start them individually (as they are standalone applications). As you install programs with Anaconda, additional menu items become available under the Anaconda menu tree for each of the applications to run directly. The menu item has coding to start the individual applications as needed.

As you can see in the preceding screen, the **Home** display shows the applications available. There are additional menu choices for:

- **Environments**: This menu displays all the Python packages that have been installed. I don't think R packages are displayed, nor are other tools or packages included in this display.
- **Projects (beta)**: This menu is usually empty. I have been using/upgrading Anaconda for a while and have not seen anything displayed here.
- **Learning**: This is a very useful feature, where a number of tutorials, videos, and write-ups have been included for the different applications that you (may) have installed.
- **Community**: This lists some community groups for the different products you have installed.

The preceding screen shows Jupyter as an installed program. The standard install of Anaconda does include Jupyter. If you choose not to use Anaconda, you can install Jupyter directly.

Installing Jupyter directly

Jupyter, as a project, grew out of Python, so it is somewhat dependent on which version of Python you have installed. For Python 2 installations, the command line steps to install Jupyter are:

```
python -m pip install --upgrade pip
python -m pip install jupyter
```

This assumes you have `pip` installed. The `pip` system is a package management system written in Python. To install `pip` on your Windows machine, execute the following line:

```
python get-pip.py
```

As you can see, this is all Python (this code calls Python to execute a standard Python script).

Installing Jupyter through Anaconda

Anaconda provides the tools to install a number of programs, including Jupyter. Once you have installed Anaconda, Jupyter will be available to you already.

The only issue I found was that the engine installed was Python 2 instead of Python 3. There is a process that Anaconda uses to decide which version of Python to run on your machine. In my case, I started out with Python 2. To upgrade to Python 3, I used these commands:

```
conda create -n py3k python=3
anaconda source activate py3k
ipython kernelspec install-self
```

After this, when you start Jupyter, you will have the Python 3 engine choice.

You may prefer to have the Python 2 engine also available. This might be if you want to use scripts that were written using Python 2. The commands to add Python 2 back in as an engine choice are:

```
python2 -m pip install ipykernel
python2 -m ipykernel install --user
```

You should now see Python 2 and Python 3 as engine choices when you start Jupyter:

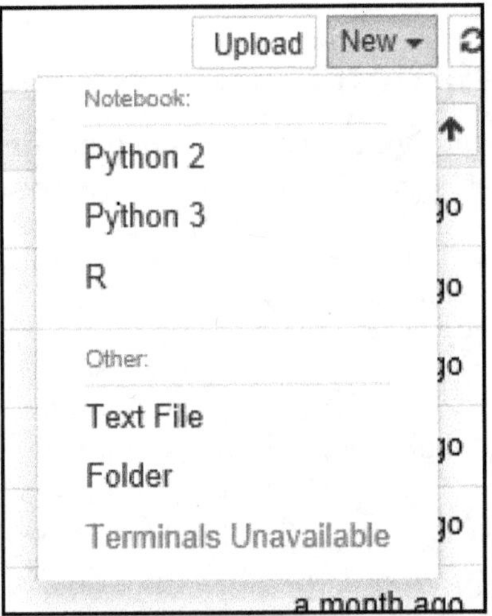

Installing Jupyter on the Mac

Apple Macintosh provides a graphical interface that runs on the OS/X operating system. OS/X includes running BSD under the hood. BSD is a version of Unix originally developed at Berkeley. As a version of Unix, it has all the standard developer tools expected by Jupyter to install and upgrade the software; they are built-in tools.

Getting ready

Jupyter can be installed on the Mac using Anaconda (as before for Windows) or via the command line.

How to do it...

In this section, we will go through the steps for installing Jupyter on Mac.

Installing Jupyter on the Mac via Anaconda

Just as with Windows earlier, we download the latest version of Anaconda and run the installation program. One of the screens should look like this:

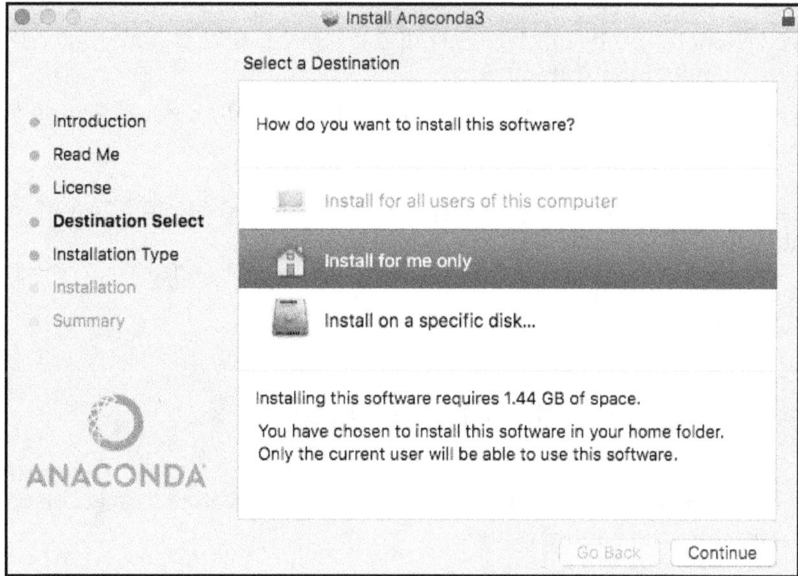

The Anaconda install is very typical for Mac installs: users can run the program and make sure they want to allocate so much storage for the application to install.

Once installed, Jupyter (and **Anaconda Navigator**) is available just like any other application on the system. You can run Jupyter directly, or you can launch Jupyter from the **Anaconda Navigator** display.

Installing Jupyter on the the Mac via the command line

Many Mac users will prefer using the command line to install Jupyter. Using the command line, you can decide whether to install Jupyter with the Python 2 or Python 3 engine. If you want to add the Python 2 engine as a choice in Jupyter, you can follow similar steps for doing so in the earlier Windows command line installation section.

The script to install Jupyter on Mac via the command line with the Python 3 engine is:

```
bash ~/Downloads/Anaconda3-5.0.0-MacOSX-x86_64.sh
```

Similarly, the command to install with the Python 2 engine is as follows:

```
bash ~/Downloads/Anaconda2-5.0.0-MacOSX-x86_64.sh
```

In either case, you will be prompted by some regular install questions:

- Review and agree to the license agreement
- Specify whether the standard install directory is OK (if not, you can specify where to install the software)
- Specify whether to prepend the Anaconda location in your user path (Anaconda recommends this step)

At this point, you should be able to start Jupyter with the command line and see the appropriate engine choice available:

```
jupyter notebook
```

Installing Jupyter on Linux

Linux is one of the easier installations for Jupyter. Linux has all the tools required to update Jupyter going forward. For Linux, we use similar commands to those shown earlier to install on the Mac from the command line.

How to do it...

Linux is a very common platform for most programming tasks. Many of the tools used in programming have been developed on Linux and later ported to other operating systems, such as Windows.

We are using Anaconda to install on Linux, but the graphical interface is not available.

The script to install Jupyter on Linux via the command line with the Python 3 engine is:

```
bash ~/Downloads/Anaconda3-5.0.0.1-Linux-x86_64.sh
```

Similarly, the command to install with the Python 2 engine is:

```
bash ~/Downloads/Anaconda2-5.0.0.1-Linux-x86_64.sh
```

In either case, you will be prompted by some regular install questions:

- Review and agree to the license agreement
- Specify whether the standard install directory is OK (if not, you can specify where to install the software)
- Specify whether to prepend the Anaconda location in your user path (Anaconda recommends this step)

And, as shown earlier under specify Windows and Mac installation sections, you can have the Python 2 and Python 3 engines available using similar steps.

At this point, you should be able to start **Anaconda Navigator** with the command line:

```
anaconda-navigator
```

Or you can run Jupyter directly using the regular command line:

```
jupyter notebook
```

Installing Jupyter on a server

The term **server** has changed over time to mean several things. We are interested in a machine that will have multiple users accessing the same software concurrently. Jupyter Notebooks can be run by multiple users. However, there is no facility to separate the data for one user from another. Standard Jupyter installations only expect and account for one user. If we have a Notebook that allows for data input from the user, then the data from different users will be intermingled in one instance and possibly displayed incorrectly.

How to do it...

See the following example in this section.

Example Notebook with a user data collision

We can see an example of a collision with a Notebook that allows for data entry from a user and responds with incorrect results:

- I call upon an example that I have used elsewhere for illustration. For this example, we will use a simple Notebook that asks the user for some information and changes the display to use that information:

```
from ipywidgets import interact
def myfunction(x):
    return x
interact(myfunction, x= "Hello World ");
```

- The script presents a textbox to the user, with the original value of the box containing the `Hello World` string.
- As the user interacts with the input field and changes the value, the value of the variable `x` in the script changes accordingly and is displayed on screen. For example, I have changed the value to the letter `A`:

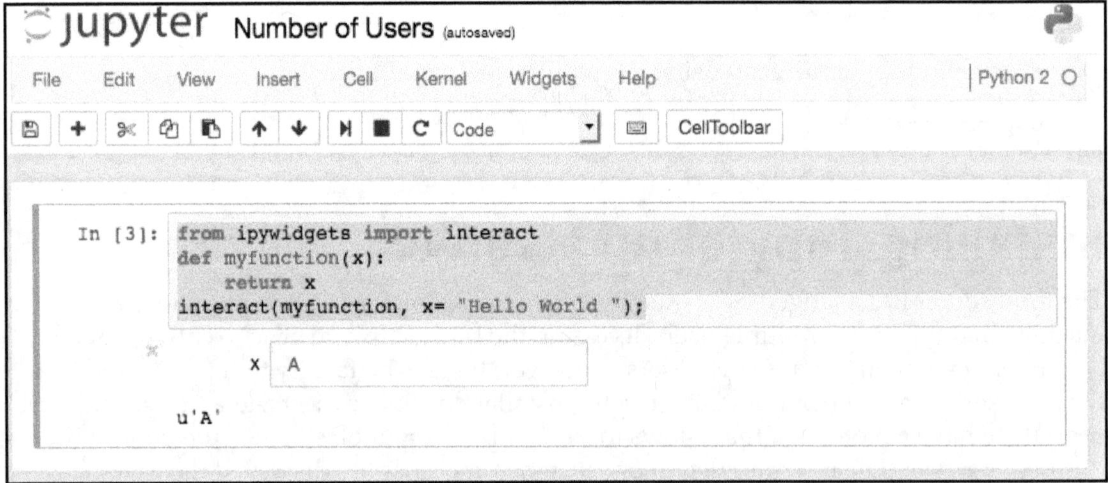

- We can see the multiuser problem if we open the same page in another browser window (copy the URL, open a new browser window, paste in the URL, and hit *Enter*). We get the exact same display—which is incorrect. We expected the new window to start with a new script, just prompting us with the default `Hello World` message. However, since the Jupyter software expects only one user, there is only one copy of the variable `x`; thus, it displays its value `A`.

We can have a Notebook server that expects multiple users and separates their instances from each other without the annoying collisions occurring. A Notebook server includes the standard Jupyter Notebook application that we have seen, but a server can also include software to distinguish the data of one user from another. We'll cover several examples of this solution in `Chapter 8`, *Multiuser Environments*.

2
Adding an Engine

In this chapter, we will cover the following recipes:

- Adding the Python 3 engine
- Adding the R engine
- Adding the Julia engine
- Adding the JavaScript engine
- Adding the Scala engine
- Adding the Spark engine

Introduction

Jupyter provides the ability to use a variety of languages when developing a Notebook. Each of the languages is supported through the use of an engine that provides all of the programmatic interface from the coded language instruction that you write with the underlying Notebook. Several of the popular languages in use are Python, R, Julia, JavaScript, and Scala. In this chapter, we will show you the steps to add these engines to your Jupyter installation so that you can script your Notebook in the language you like.

Each Notebook is expected to be written using one language per engine. There are some accommodations for mixing languages in one Notebook, but these are not expected to have a large amount of use.

Adding the Python 3 engine

Jupyter was originally derived from Python with the IPython project. At that time, Python 2 was the predominant version available for use. For every installation of Jupyter, the default engine provided is Python 2. There are a number of changes involved when moving from Python 2 to Python 3, especially in the underlying libraries that you may be invoking, where parameter and usage changes have occurred.

How to do it...

We will cover the installation of the Python 3 engine and make sure it is running with a script.

Installing the Python 3 engine

Assuming you have installed the standard Jupyter package, you now have Python 2 as the only engine available at the top of the Jupyter portal screen:

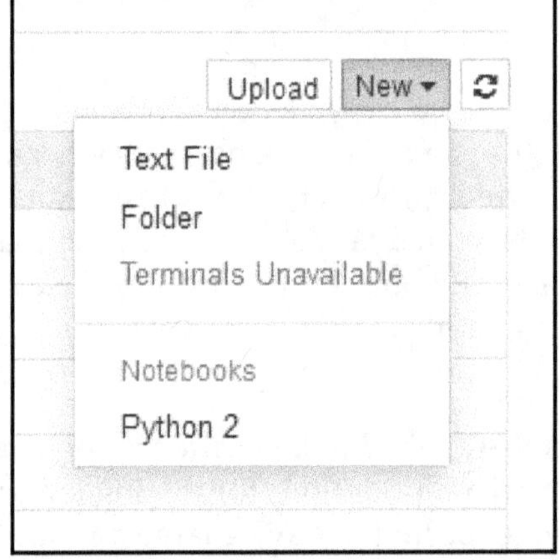

To upgrade to Python 3, I used the commands:

```
conda create -n py3k python=3
anaconda source activate py3k
ipython kernelspec install-self
```

After this, when you start Jupyter, you will have the Python 3 engine choice.

You may prefer to have the Python 2 engine also available. This could be if you want to use scripts that were written using Python 2.

The commands to add Python 2 back in as an engine choice are:

```
python2 -m pip install ipykernel
python2 -m ipykernel install --user
```

You should now see Python 2 and Python 3 as engine choices when you start Jupyter:

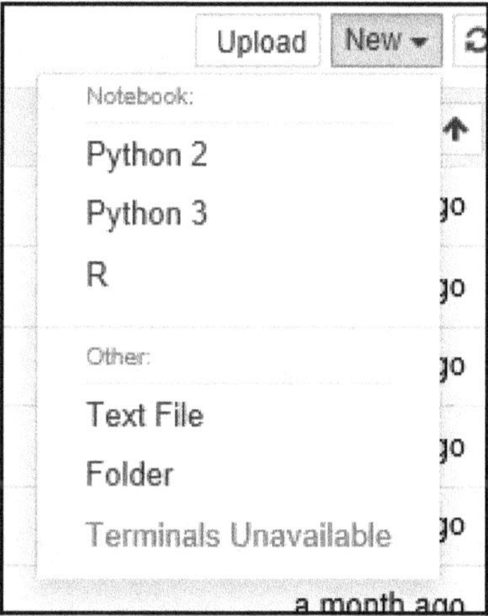

Running a Python 3 script

We can see that we truly have Python 3 by making a small Notebook entry, using the Python 3 engine:

```
print("Hello World")
```

The use of parentheses around the `print` argument is a syntactical change in Python 3. We can see this execute in our Notebook:

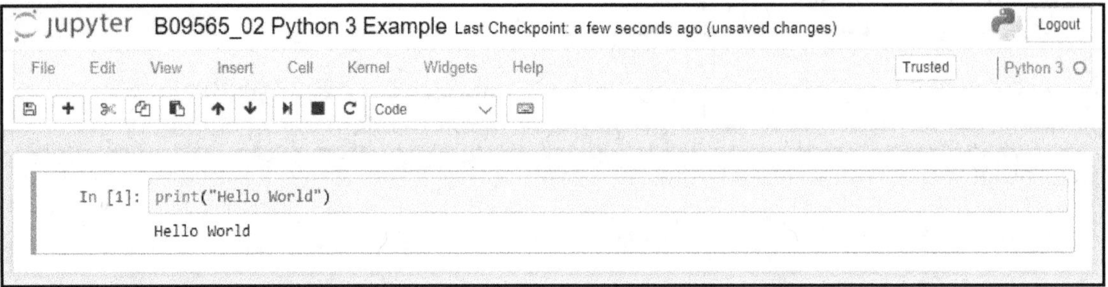

Adding the R engine

R is both a programming language and a software environment geared toward statistical computing and associated graphics. R has a clean syntax, providing access to a large set of statistical packages, publicly available for free use.

How to do it...

We can add the R engine to our Jupyter installation using Anaconda Navigator or the command line.

Installing the R engine using Anaconda Navigator

R is included with the R Studio option in Anaconda Navigator, as shown in this partial screenshot:

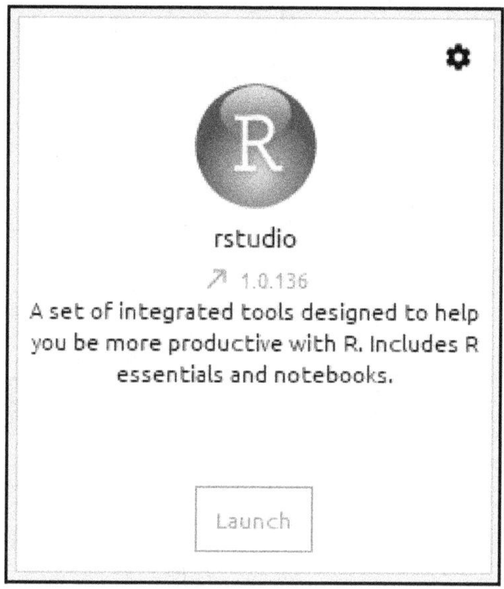

As noted in the screen, the R Studio installation includes R essentials and Notebooks (Notebook engine support).

This screenshot shows R after it has been installed (see the **Launch** button). Whereas before it is installed, the **rstudio** graphic icon will display in Anaconda Navigator with an **Install** button.

Once you select the **Install** button, Anaconda will automatically install R in your environment and bring you back to the Navigator screen, now showing the **Launch** button as shown in the preceding screenshot.

Installing the R engine via command line

If you decide to add the R engine using the command line, you can use the following command:

```
conda install r-essentials
```

It is usually a good idea to update regularly as well, using this command:

```
conda update r-essentials
```

Once we have installed R as an engine choice, we can create a new R Notebook from the **New** menu dropdown, as shown in this screenshot:

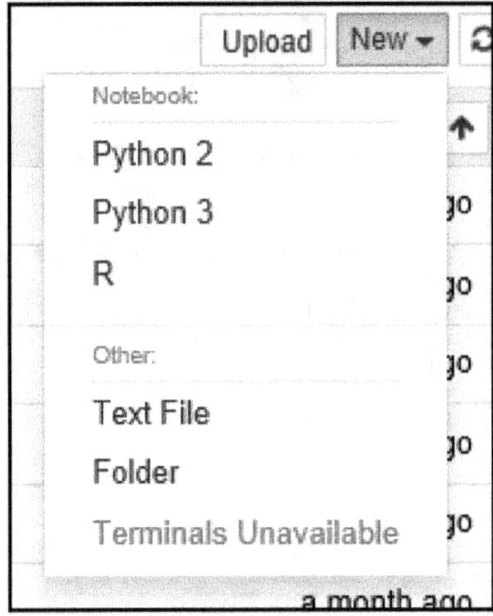

Running an R Script

We can now run an R script in our R Notebook using the following script lines to prove that our installation is complete:

```
name <- "Dan Toomey"
print(paste("Hello World", name))
```

With the resulting screen as:

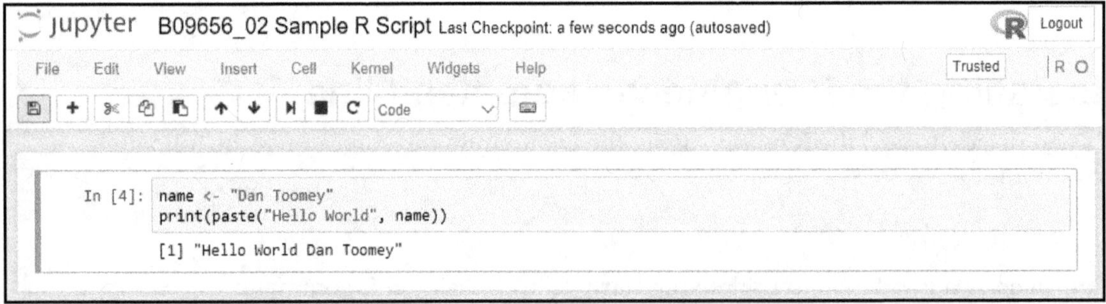

Adding the Julia engine

Julia is a high-level programming language. It was built with high performance in mind, especially with regard to numerical computing. As such, it is a custom-made language for data science use.

How to do it...

We will now cover the steps to add the Julia engine and execute a Julia script under Jupyter.

Installing the Julia engine

I know that in previous instances of Jupyter, Julia was automatically installed as an engine in non-Windows environments. I do not have access to another environment, so we will walk through the steps to installing Julia on Windows.

The first step is to download and install the appropriate version from the Julia downloads page, `https://julialang.org/downloads`. I noticed that there are installs available for macOS and Linux from this page as well. In my case, I could use the 64-bit self-extracting executable. Once installed, we can start the Julia environment, which has a splash screen like this:

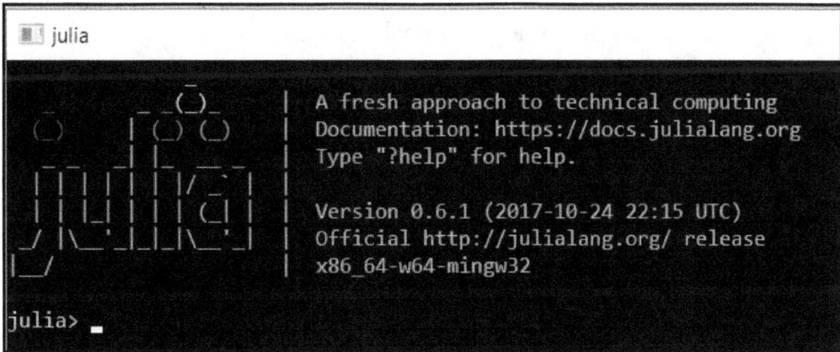

Now that Julia is installed, we can request the `IJulia` package to be loaded in. `IJulia` is the Julia engine for Jupyter. `IJulia` provides the linkage of the Julia script we entered in the Notebook with the Julia environment. We enter the Julia command:

```
Pkg.add("IJulia")
```

It's shown in this screenshot:

```
julia> Pkg.add("IJulia")
INFO: Initializing package repository C:\Users\Dan\.julia\v0.6
INFO: Cloning METADATA from https://github.com/JuliaLang/METADATA.jl
INFO: Cloning cache of BinDeps from https://github.com/JuliaLang/BinDeps.jl.git
INFO: Cloning cache of BufferedStreams from https://github.com/BioJulia/BufferedStreams.jl.git
INFO: Cloning cache of Compat from https://github.com/JuliaLang/Compat.jl.git
INFO: Cloning cache of Conda from https://github.com/JuliaPy/Conda.jl.git
INFO: Cloning cache of IJulia from https://github.com/JuliaLang/IJulia.jl.git
INFO: Cloning cache of JSON from https://github.com/JuliaIO/JSON.jl.git
INFO: Cloning cache of LibExpat from https://github.com/JuliaIO/LibExpat.jl.git
INFO: Cloning cache of Libz from https://github.com/BioJulia/Libz.jl.git
INFO: Cloning cache of MbedTLS from https://github.com/JuliaWeb/MbedTLS.jl.git
INFO: Cloning cache of SHA from https://github.com/staticfloat/SHA.jl.git
INFO: Cloning cache of URIParser from https://github.com/JuliaWeb/URIParser.jl.git
INFO: Cloning cache of WinRPM from https://github.com/JuliaPackaging/WinRPM.jl.git
INFO: Cloning cache of ZMQ from https://github.com/JuliaInterop/ZMQ.jl.git
INFO: Installing BinDeps v0.7.0
```

Note that there are many pieces that get installed as part of this installation. The preceding screenshot is just the first part of the display.

We now have Julia installed as an engine, and we will see **Julia 0.6.1** as an engine choice in Jupyter, as shown in the following screenshot:

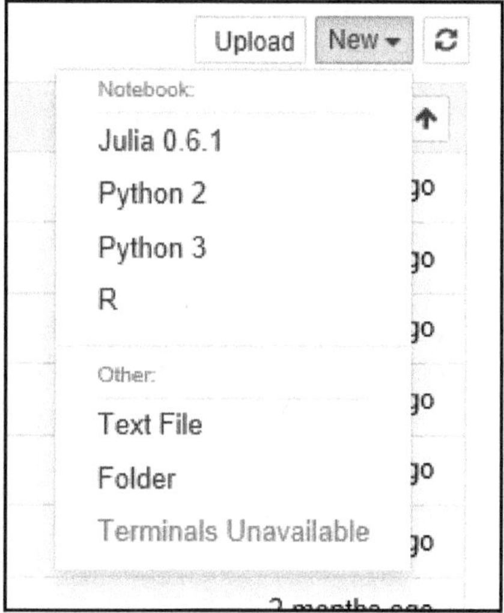

Running a Julia script

Now that we have Julia installed and the engine added to Jupyter, we can see a sample script run in a Julia Notebook, such as this:

```
Pkg.add("RDatasets")
using RDatasets
describe(dataset("datasets", "iris"))
```

This script loads in `RDatasets` (this contains several standard datasets commonly used in data science). It then runs the Julia `describe` command on the `iris` dataset.

We would only need to add the `RDatasets` package once. Adding this package will download a number of entries.

This is resultant display:

```
In [2]: Pkg.add("RDatasets")
        using RDatasets
        describe(dataset("datasets", "iris"))

        INFO: Cloning cache of DataArrays from https://github.com/Julia
        INFO: Cloning cache of DataFrames from https://github.com/Julia
        INFO: Cloning cache of DataStructures from https://github.com/J
        INFO: Cloning cache of FileIO from https://github.com/JuliaIO/F
        INFO: Cloning cache of GZip from https://github.com/JuliaIO/GZi
        INFO: Cloning cache of RData from https://github.com/JuliaStats
        INFO: Cloning cache of RDatasets from https://github.com/johnmy
        INFO: Cloning cache of Reexport from https://github.com/simonst
        INFO: Cloning cache of SortingAlgorithms from https://github.co
        INFO: Cloning cache of SpecialFunctions from https://github.com
        INFO: Cloning cache of StatsBase from https://github.com/JuliaS
        INFO: Installing DataArrays v0.6.2
        INFO: Installing DataFrames v0.10.1
        INFO: Installing DataStructures v0.7.2
        INFO: Installing FileIO v0.5.2
        INFO: Installing GZip v0.3.0
        INFO: Installing RData v0.1.0
        INFO: Installing RDatasets v0.2.0
        INFO: Installing Reexport v0.0.3
        INFO: Installing SortingAlgorithms v0.1.1
        INFO: Installing SpecialFunctions v0.3.4
        INFO: Installing StatsBase v0.19.0
        INFO: Building SpecialFunctions
        INFO: Package database updated
        INFO: Precompiling module Reexport.
        INFO: Precompiling module FileIO.
        INFO: Precompiling module DataFrames.
        INFO: Precompiling module RData.

        SepalLength
        Summary Stats:
        Mean:           5.843333
        Minimum:        4.300000
        1st Quartile:   5.100000
        Median:         5.800000
        3rd Quartile:   6.400000
        Maximum:        7.900000
        Length:         150
        Type:           Float64
        Number Missing: 0
        % Missing:      0.000000
```

This display continues for the rest of the items in the iris dataset.

The series of **INFO** debug lines in the output occurs as Julia is deciding to install/update dependent packages to execute your script. If no dependency changes are detected, they will not be shown.

Adding the JavaScript engine

JavaScript is another engine that can be used with Jupyter. Actually, it is `node.js` rather than JavaScript. `node.js` is a superset of JavaScript. `node.js` is an extension of JavaScript that is expected to be run on a server. As with JavaScript, `node.js` is cross-platform.

How to do it...

We will go over the steps to install the engine and run a small script.

Installing the Node.JS engine

First, we need to install `node.js`. It is available from `node.js.org`. From this site, you can download and install `node.js` on your machine directly. The installer for Windows is a standard design that looks similar for other environments.

Next, we need to install the JavaScript engine, `ijavascript`. We use the `npm` tool (installed with `node.js`) to install `ijavascript` with the command:

```
npm install -g ijavascript
```

The non-Windows running of this script is within `sudo` (the `run` command as a superuser), so I think the equivalent would be to run this script from a command window that is run as administrator in Windows.

The `ijavascript` command includes several features; of particular interest is the `ijsinstall` tool. The `ijsinstall` adds the `ijavascript` engine to Jupyter. So, from the command line, we can run this command:

```
ijsinstall
```

At this point we have JavaScript as an engine choice, as can be seen in this screenshot:

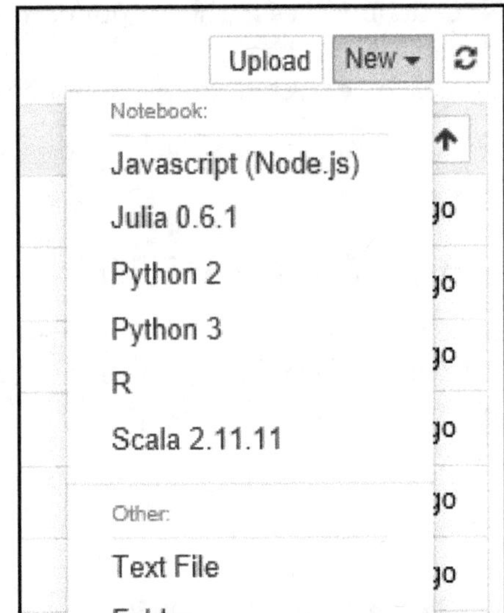

Showing the JavaScript (node.js) engine choice

However, the `node.js` engine expects an older version of Jupyter to be hosted. So, every time you start your JavaScript Notebook, you will get an engine failure with a modern version of Jupyter. This may not be the case with non-Windows installations.

Running a Node.JS script

I had run such a script in a prior version of Jupyter on another machine as I was able to see these results with the small script:

```
var msg = "Hello, World"
console.log(msg)
```

With the resultant screen display as:

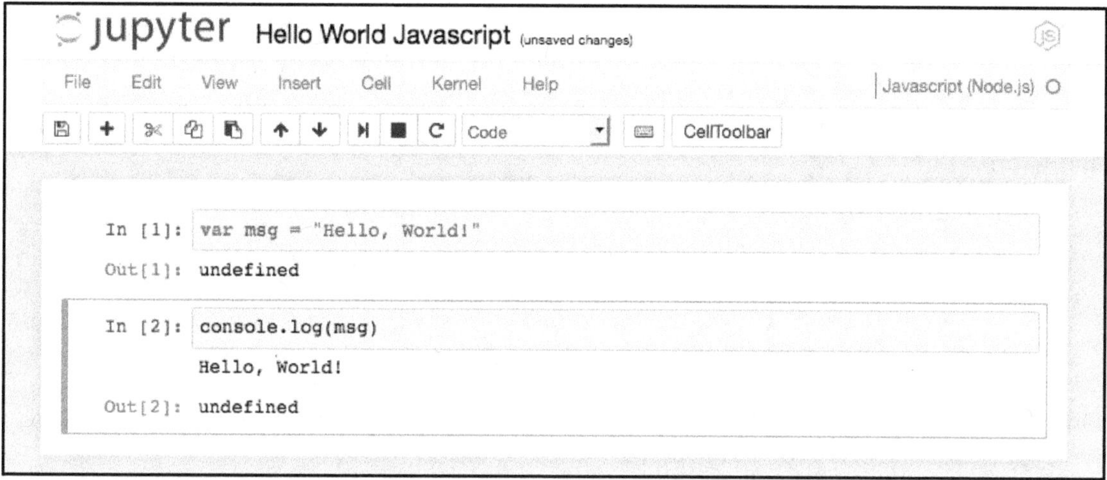

Adding the Scala engine

Scala is described as a general-use language that is concise and elegant. Scala is an extension of the Java language and can call upon Java libraries. Its syntax is very similar as well.

How to do it...

We now go over the steps to install the Scala engine and run a Scala script.

Installing the Scala engine

The Scala engine implementation is immature. There may be better installations available for non-Windows environments, but for Windows I followed the following instructions, where someone had built a version of the Scala engine for Windows that you can add to your environment.

At the bottom of this issue on the Jupyter Scala board at `https://github.com/jupyter-scala/jupyter-scala/issues/108`, there is a link to the code that you can use. At the bottom of that issue is the actual link: `https://github.com/jupyter-scala/jupyter-scala/issues/1#issuecomment-315643483`. Here, someone has set up a Scala engine for Windows to download at `https://github.com/rvilla87/Big-Data/raw/master/other/jupyter-Scala_2.11.11_kernel_Windows.zip`. Unpack this `.zip` file. The `README` file has instructions for:

- Copying the Scala engine into your environment.
- Editing the engine JSON file (included in the Scala engine previously) to point to this directory again. For me, the line changed to `C:\\Users\\Dan\\Anaconda3\\share\\jupyter\\kernels\\scala\\launcher.jar` as I am attempting to use Anaconda for all Jupyter work.

Once you have copied in the files and made the preceding change, you should see Scala as an engine choice when you start Jupyter:

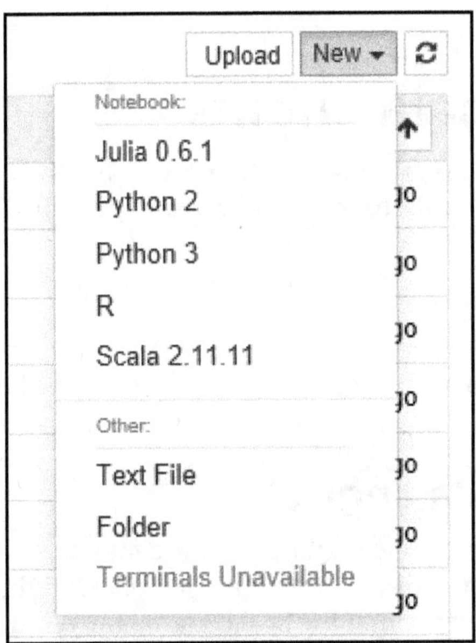

Running a Scala script

We can see a simple `Hello World` output using Scala with this script:

```
println("Hello World")
```

It shows up in a Scala Notebook as:

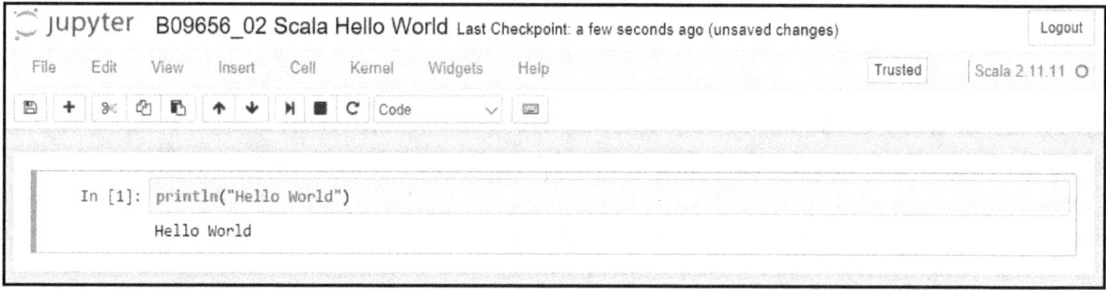

Adding the Spark engine

Spark is an Apache project that provides an open source computing framework specially geared toward cluster computing. For our purposes, it provides a language called **Spark** that can be used to access Hadoop information sets.

How to do it...

We install the Spark engine and execute a Spark Jupyter script to show its working, as follows.

Installing the Spark engine

Generally, installing Spark involves two steps:

- Installing Spark (for your environment)
- Connecting Spark to your environment (whether standalone or clustered)

The Spark installations are environment specific. I've included the steps to install Spark (in connection with Jupyter) for a Windows environment here. There are different instructions for other environments.

Similarly, Spark relies on a base language to work from. This can be Scala or Python. We automatically have Python as part of the Jupyter installations, so we will rely on Python as the basis. In other words, we will code a Python Notebook, where Python statements invoke Spark libraries to perform different steps.

Steps for installing:

1. Download and unpack the latest Spark version from `http://spark.apache.org/downloads`. Unpack the TGZ file and copy the underlying directory to `C:\spark` (the directory name needs to match exactly the following instruction).
2. We need to provide environment-dependent tools for Spark to use. These are packaged as `winutils.exe` available at `http://public-repo-1.hortonworks.com/hdp-win-alpha/winutils.exe`. Download the `.exe`, file and move it into the `C:\winutils` directory.
3. Set the environment variables for Spark to work with:
    - `HADOOP_HOME=C:\winutils`
    - `SPARK_HOME=C:\spark`
    - `PYSPARK_DRIVER_PYTHON=ipython`
    - `PYSPARK_DRIVER_PYTHON_OPTS=notebook`

Running a Spark script

We can run a small Spark script to read in a file and sum up the line lengths. We are using `lambda` functions to map/reduce the sizes in a Hadoop fashion:

```
import pyspark
if not 'sc' in globals():
    sc = pyspark.SparkContext()
lines = sc.textFile("B09656_02 Spark Sample.ipynb")
lineLengths = lines.map(lambda s: len(s))
totalLengths = lineLengths.reduce(lambda a, b: a + b)
print(totalLengths)
```

That results in a screen that looks like this:

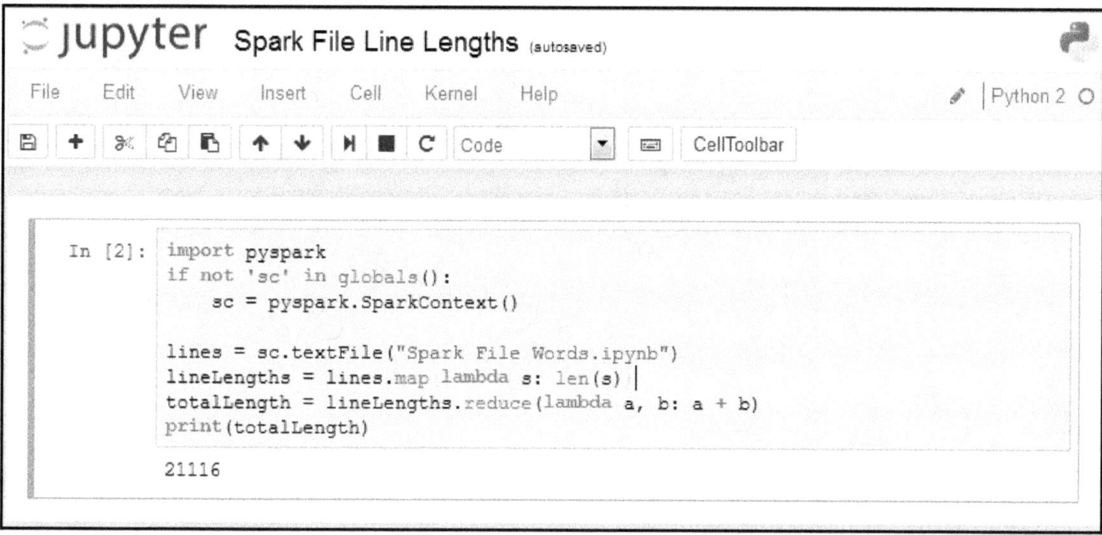

Note that we are running a Python 2 Notebook that calls upon the Spark (`pyspark`) library.

3
Accessing and Retrieving Data

In this chapter, we will cover the following recipes:

- Reading CSV files
- Reading JSON files
- Accessing a database
- Reading flat files
- Reading text files

Introduction

There is a wide variety of data source file formats in use. Luckily, most of the languages that we can use in Jupyter support these formats. Some languages are idiosyncratic in the format of the resultant dataset once loaded into memory, and some even allow keeping only one record at a time in memory to avoid overwhelming it. It will help you to have data in other formats; in acquisition data, we need to have different formats for new data, and these will be applied when reading files.

Reading CSV files

The most common file format for datasets is a **comma separated value** (**CSV**) file. A CSV may have a header record followed by a variable number of data records.

The header record may be the first record in the file. In that record, the separated values are headings or column names for each of the columns of data in the file. The column names are all character string values. We can use these column names for variable names in our scripts, corresponding to column names in a dataset.

Each subsequent data record will have a separated value in that record for every column. The value may be an empty string or no value, but the comma separation of the record will correspond to the columns in the header record.

If there is no header record, you may have to find out what the column layout is for the file. There is normally a descriptor in the same location as the CSV file that describes each of the columns. In this case, you have to manually assign column names to your working dataset, according to the descriptor document.

You can load a CSV directly into a spreadsheet program, such as Excel. Excel will split out the columns based on commas. Note that the number of records may exceed the space available for Excel (usually 64K records), but it will at least load the initial records of your file. It is usually a good idea to load your CSV into a spreadsheet to validate that the format and column types are as expected.

Getting ready

In all cases, we need direct access to the CSV file for our script to work. The CSV file may reside on the internet as most languages support accessing a file over the internet. However, if there is a login procedure before accessing the file, you will have to download the CSV file to a local disk in order to access it. There is normally no provision to provide login credentials before accessing a file over the internet in our scripts.

How to do it...

We will show how to access a CSV file using R. This and the other languages available in Jupyter work in a very similar manner.

For this example, I will be accessing the heating data from `https://raw.github.com/vincentarelbundock/Rdatasets/master/csv/Ecdat/Heating.csv`. In my case, I have downloaded the file to access it locally (I was developing the access on a train ride and was unclear about the internet access). This file has costs for different heating choices made by homeowners in California.

We can read in the file to a DataFrame using the `read.csv` command:

```
heating <-
read.csv(file="https://raw.github.com/vincentarelbundock/Rdatasets/master/c
sv/Ecdat/Heating.csv", header=TRUE, sep=",")
```

The resulting DataFrame is named `heating`. The filename is the location of the file to read. In this case, the file does have a header record. This is a true CSV, so the separator is a comma. Interestingly, the `read.csv` command accounts for other separators to be used instead of a comma. A common alternate character to use is *Tab*, which would be scripted as `\t`, meaning the backslash to note the following character is to be interpreted rather than taken literally. And the `t` is a universal code for *Tab*.

I would normally display the first few records once I have loaded a file. Again, a visual validation that we have the correct file information.

R has the built-in function `head`, which does just that so we can see the following output:

```
head(heating)
```

This is the resulting display of the DataFrame:

In [2]: head(heating)

X	idcase	depvar	ic.gc	ic.gr	ic.ec	ic.er	ic.hp	oc.gc	oc.gr	...	oc.hp	income	agehed
1	1	gc	866.00	962.64	859.90	995.76	1135.50	199.69	151.72	...	237.88	7	25
2	2	gc	727.93	758.89	796.82	894.69	968.90	168.66	168.66	...	199.19	5	60
3	3	gc	599.48	783.05	719.86	900.11	1048.30	165.58	137.80	...	171.47	4	65
4	4	er	835.17	793.06	761.25	831.04	1048.70	180.88	147.14	...	222.95	2	50
5	5	er	755.59	846.29	858.86	985.64	883.05	174.91	138.90	...	178.49	2	25
6	6	gc	666.11	841.71	693.74	862.56	859.18	135.67	140.97	...	209.27	6	65

You should notice the ellipsis in the middle of each row, denoting that there are more columns in the data than can fit on the screen. The other aspect to note is the column names are not very meaningful. We can look at the documentation (in the `.doc` file in the same internet directory) to determine some column names that are more meaningful. We can change the column names accordingly using the `colnames` command:

```
# change the column names to be more readable
 colnames(heating)[colnames(heating)=="depvar"] <- "system"
 colnames(heating)[colnames(heating)=="ic.gc"] <- "install_cost"
 colnames(heating)[colnames(heating)=="oc.gc"] <- "annual_cost"
 colnames(heating)[colnames(heating)=="pb.gc"] <- "ratio_annual_install"
```

We can also see from the documentation that a number of columns are really not of much interest to us; so we can remove them from our dataset by just assigning their value to `NULL` (similar commands are available in all languages to drop a column from a dataset):

```
# remove unused columns
heating$idcase <- NULL
heating$ic.gr <- NULL
heating$ic.ec <- NULL
heating$ic.hp <- NULL
heating$ic.er <- NULL
heating$oc.gr <- NULL
heating$oc.ec <- NULL
heating$oc.hp <- NULL
heating$oc.er <- NULL
heating$pb.gr <- NULL
heating$pb.ec <- NULL
heating$pb.er <- NULL
heating$pb.hp <- NULL
```

Now, if we display our first few records, the information will be more presentable and useful:

```
head(heating)
```

The output of the preceding code is as follows:

```
In [7]: head(heating)
```

X	system	install_cost	annual_cost	income	agehed	rooms	region	ratio_annual_install
1	gc	866.00	199.69	7	25	6	ncostl	4.336722
2	gc	727.93	168.66	5	60	5	scostl	4.315961
3	gc	599.48	165.58	4	65	2	ncostl	3.620486
4	er	835.17	180.88	2	50	4	scostl	4.617260
5	er	755.59	174.91	2	25	6	valley	4.319879
6	gc	666.11	135.67	6	65	7	scostl	4.909781

How it works...

So, we made sure we had access to the file where we could have downloaded to a local space, if necessary.

We were able to verify the file is as expected using Excel (or some other spreadsheet product). We could have loaded into a text file editor as well, but the display would not have shown the column layouts inherently.

We then used a built-in command to read the file into a data format of use. In this case, the R command was `read.csv` and the data format was a DataFrame. We changed the column names and removed unused columns to conform to our needs.

A further option available for `read.csv` (and supported in other languages) is to ignore records containing `NA` values. There are many datasets available that have this condition—some `NA` values are present. You can decide whether the results are worth navigating around the `NA` values or you want to just drop those records from your processing.

Reading JSON files

The modern approach to file formats is to use **JavaScript Object Notation** (**JSON**). It was specifically developed for interpretation by JavaScript coding, typically in a website. For example, a web page needs a list of products and asks for that list from the web server coding. The web server coding responds with the information encoded in JSON format, knowing that JavaScript resides in the web application and can easily interpret the information.

As it became more popular to use JSON on web applications, many realized it was a robust data format supporting hierarchical structures without having to resort to the flattening required by CSV. People then started using JSON in a variety of applications, not just website intercommunication.

Getting ready

We need to locate a JSON file of reasonable complexity. There are many. You will see in most of the standard repositories for datasets that a good sprinkling of JSON format files is now available. In this example, I am referencing the list of Ford models from `http://www.carqueryapi.com/api/0.3/?callback=?cmd=getModelsmake=ford`. I could not reference this directly as it is not a flat file, but an API call. So, I downloaded the data into a local file, `fords.json`. There were a few extra characters at the beginning and the end of the download. Once I had removed those, I used an online pretty print program to validate the format of the `.json`, as shown in this screenshot:

```
{
    "Models": [
        {
            "model_name": "021 C",
            "model_make_id": "ford"
        },
        {
            "model_name": "12 M",
            "model_make_id": "ford"
        },
```

A pretty print program takes a raw source file, in this case a JSON file, and displays it in a presentable and attractive manner. This is useful as the raw format is usually one long line of text.

While we can use most languages to read our JSON, the best configuration is likely to be by using JavaScript. JavaScript is one of the language choices available for our Notebook. If you prefer another language, you can run two scripts. First run script 1 to load in the JSON using JavaScript, and then store an intermediate format for use by script 2 in your favorite language. But again, other languages do support JSON; it is just more cumbersome to do so.

How to do it...

We can use JavaScript to read in the JSON, walk through the list of vehicles, gather some simple statistics, and print out on the screen.

The script we are using is:

```
//load the JSON dataset
//http://www.carqueryapi.com/api/0.3/?callback=?&cmd=getModels&make=ford
var fords = require('/Users/dtoomey/fords.json');
//display how many Ford models are in our data set
console.log("There are " + fords.Models.length + " Ford models in the data
set");
//loop over the set
var index = 1
for(var i=0; i<fords.Models.length; i++) {
    //get this model
    var model = fords.Models[i];
   //pull it's name
    var name = model.model_name;
    //if the model name does not have numerics in it
    if(! name.match(/[0-9]/i)) {
        //display the model name
        console.log("Model " + index + " is a " + name);
        index++;
    }
   //only display the first 5
   if (index>5) break;
}
```

We can see this in our Notebook as:

```
//load the JSON dataset
//http://www.carqueryapi.com/api/0.3/?callback=?&cmd=getModels&make=ford
var fords = require('/Users/dtoomey/fords.json');

//display how many Ford models are in our data set
console.log("There are " + fords.Models.length + " Ford models in the data set");

//loop over the set
var index = 1
for(var i=0; i<fords.Models.length; i++) {

    //get this model
    var model = fords.Models[i];

    //pull it's name
    var name = model.model_name;

    //if the model name does not have numerics in it
    if(! name.match(/[0-9]/i)) {
        //display the model name
        console.log("Model " + index + " is a " + name);
        index++;
    }

    //only display the first 5
    if (index>5) break;
}
```

And when run, we get the output expected as:

```
           There are 147 Ford models in the data set
           Model 1 is a Aerostar
           Model 2 is a Anglia
           Model 3 is a Artic
           Model 4 is a Aspire
           Model 5 is a Bantam

Out[27]:   5
```

How it works...

The script first loads in the JSON just by using `require`. `require` is normally used for including code snippets for easy reusability, but it does the same thing, that is, loads a block of text into memory. We assign this block of text to the variable `fords`.

Since the required file ends with JSON, JavaScript automatically assumes it to be actually a JSON-formatted file and parses out the components of the file accordingly. As we can see in the preceding pretty print display, the file is composed of the Ford models, where each model has an internal Ford model name and a make that the public is aware of.

`Model` is an array of vehicle information. Arrays can be accessed by an index, such as `array[0]`, `array[1]`, and so on. Arrays have built-in attributes (such as the size of an array) and functionality (such as adding records to an array). We use the array size to first print out how many records are in the array.

We construct a `for` loop with `i` as our index and access each model. We are looking for the first five modes that do not have a number in their model name. So, we test the name for numbers using pattern matching. If the name is only alphabetical, we print out the name and increment our counter.

At the end of every loop, we check whether we have five vehicles yet, and stop if we do.

Accessing a database

Much information is available over the internet, but some of the more sensitive or private information is available in corporate and government databases only. Fortunately, many of the languages in Jupyter provide mechanisms to access data from a database.

For this example, we will be using R for scripting. R has a database connection library, `dbplyr`, that can be used to access some of the more common databases. As with the file loads elsewhere in this chapter, the result of a database read would be a DataFrame. Once there, you can operate on the DataFrame like any other.

Some of the other Jupyter languages have database support through a library as well. In particular, Python and Scala have database access. In general, they work in the same manner:

1. Make a connection to the database
2. Run a query on the database that returns a result set
3. The library converts the result set into a usable data type for the language

Note: some libraries allow you to work as much as possible on the database side before downloading to your script. In other words, build up a result set on the database, manipulate that result set as needed, and finally download the data to your script.

Getting ready

For this example, I could have installed one of several databases, but an even easier solution is to use SQLite, which comes embedded automatically as part of one of the R libraries. Then we create the database in memory so that we do not have to account for operating system differences for file handling.

How to do it...

To install and load the libraries, we will use:

```
install.packages("dbplyr", repos='http://cran.us.r-project.org')
install.packages("RSQLite", repos='http://cran.us.r-project.org')
library(dplyr)
library(RSQLite)

# connect (and create) our in memory database
 con <- DBI::dbConnect(RSQLite::SQLite(), path = ":memory:")

# load the iris dataset
 install.packages("datasets", repos='http://cran.us.r-project.org')
 library(datasets)
 data(iris)
 summary(iris)
```

You will get the following result:

```
  Sepal.Length    Sepal.Width     Petal.Length    Petal.Width   
 Min.   :4.300   Min.   :2.000   Min.   :1.000   Min.   :0.100  
 1st Qu.:5.100   1st Qu.:2.800   1st Qu.:1.600   1st Qu.:0.300  
 Median :5.800   Median :3.000   Median :4.350   Median :1.300  
 Mean   :5.843   Mean   :3.057   Mean   :3.758   Mean   :1.199  
 3rd Qu.:6.400   3rd Qu.:3.300   3rd Qu.:5.100   3rd Qu.:1.800  
 Max.   :7.900   Max.   :4.400   Max.   :6.900   Max.   :2.500  
       Species  
 setosa    :50  
 versicolor:50  
 virginica :50  
```

Next we populate our database table as follows:

```
# populate a database table, iris, with the information from the iris
DataFrame
 copy_to(con, iris, "iris",
   temporary = FALSE,
   indexes = list("Species"))
 iris_db <- tbl(con, "iris")
 iris_db
```

This will give us the following result:

```
# Source:   table<iris> [?? x 5]
# Database: sqlite 3.19.3 []
   Sepal.Length Sepal.Width Petal.Length Petal.Width Species
          <dbl>       <dbl>        <dbl>       <dbl>   <chr>
 1          5.1         3.5          1.4         0.2  setosa
 2          4.9         3.0          1.4         0.2  setosa
 3          4.7         3.2          1.3         0.2  setosa
 4          4.6         3.1          1.5         0.2  setosa
 5          5.0         3.6          1.4         0.2  setosa
 6          5.4         3.9          1.7         0.4  setosa
 7          4.6         3.4          1.4         0.3  setosa
 8          5.0         3.4          1.5         0.2  setosa
 9          4.4         2.9          1.4         0.2  setosa
10          4.9         3.1          1.5         0.1  setosa
# ... with more rows
```

```
# notice there is nothing on the R side yet
nrow(iris_db)
[1] NA

head(iris_db, n=10)
```

You will get the following output:

```
In [21]: head(iris_db, n = 10)

         # Source:   lazy query [?? x 5]
         # Database: sqlite 3.19.3 []
            Sepal.Length Sepal.Width Petal.Length Petal.Width Species
                   <dbl>       <dbl>        <dbl>       <dbl>   <chr>
          1          5.1         3.5          1.4         0.2  setosa
          2          4.9         3.0          1.4         0.2  setosa
          3          4.7         3.2          1.3         0.2  setosa
          4          4.6         3.1          1.5         0.2  setosa
          5          5.0         3.6          1.4         0.2  setosa
          6          5.4         3.9          1.7         0.4  setosa
          7          4.6         3.4          1.4         0.3  setosa
          8          5.0         3.4          1.5         0.2  setosa
          9          4.4         2.9          1.4         0.2  setosa
         10          4.9         3.1          1.5         0.1  setosa
         # ... with more rows
```

```
# what is sqlite doing behind the scenes
 show_query(head(iris_db, n = 10))
```

```
In [19]: show_query(head(iris_db, n = 10))

         <SQL>
         SELECT *
         FROM `iris`
         LIMIT 10
```

```
# pull data back into R using collect
 my_iris <- iris_db %>% collect()
 my_iris
```

```
In [20]: # pull data back into R using collect
         my_iris <- iris_db %>% collect()
         my_iris
```

Sepal.Length	Sepal.Width	Petal.Length	Petal.Width	Species
5.1	3.5	1.4	0.2	setosa
4.9	3.0	1.4	0.2	setosa
4.7	3.2	1.3	0.2	setosa
4.6	3.1	1.5	0.2	setosa
5.0	3.6	1.4	0.2	setosa

How it works...

We first connect (and automatically create) an in-memory database. The new database is empty. We populate a table in the empty database, using the iris dataset. There are some clear differences in operating with a database versus an R DataFrame:

- The `iris_db` display includes what the database program is running, and the column types are not as expected in R.
- We see that the `iris_db` does not reside in the R program at all—it is completely in the database. We can see that with the `NA` result from our `nrow(iris_db)` call.
- We can run a `head(iris_db)` call, and it will give results. But if you look closely, there are many database settings displayed, compared to the standard R settings.
- When we use `show_query` against an `iris_db` head function, we see that SQLite is converting what is normally an R statement into the corresponding SQL and executing that SQL against the database.

Finally, we pull the result of our database manipulation back into the R space, using the `collect` function. Now, when we display the results of the `collect`, we see normal R results.

Reading flat files

In contrast to the CSV files seen earlier, a flat file does not contain any separator between the fields. Since there is no separator, all records in a flat file are usually of the same length, as the length of columns is the only way of separating data. Prior to the advent of spreadsheet programs, it was a common practice to use only flat files. Flat files are still used according to the preference of the authors.

Getting ready

In this example, we will be using Python to read in a flat file. The `pandas` library of routines includes a function to read flat files, `read_fwf`. Your Python script passes in the column widths and names to `read_fwf`, and the function returns a DataFrame.

Of course, now that I am looking for a flat file, I can't find one! I took the first 20 records of the preceding baseball data and stored that in a flat file, `baseball.txt`. There is no header record. Only the first several columns are available. It looks like this:

```
baseball.txt - Notepad
File  Edit  Format  View  Help
  4ansonca0118711RC125120
 44forceda0118711WS332162
 68mathebo0118711FW119 89
 99startjo0118711NY233161
102suttoez0118711CL129128
106whitede0118711CL129146
113yorkto01 18711TRO29145
121ansonca0118721PH146217
143burdoja0118721BR237174
167forceda0118721TRO25130
168forceda0118722BL119 95
186hinespa0118721WS411 49
209mathebo0118721BL150223
226nelsoca0118721TRO 4 20
227nelsoca0118722BR118 76
229orourji0118721MID23101
249startjo0118721NY255282
252suttoez0118721CL122107
259whitede0118721CL122109
```

How to do it...

We can use a Python script that calls upon the pandas `read_fwf` function to read in the data file, break up the columns (according to the field widths provided), and create a DataFrame with the data:

```
import pandas as pd

column_names = ["row","id","year","stint","team","g","ab"]
column_widths = [3,9,4,1,3,2,3]
df = pd.read_fwf("c:/Users/Dan/baseball.txt",
 header=None,
 names=column_names,
 widths=column_widths)
df
```

This results in a display as follows:

Out[1]:

	row	id	year	stint	team	g	ab
0	4	ansonca01	1871	1	RC1	25	120
1	44	forceda01	1871	1	WS3	32	162
2	68	mathebo01	1871	1	FW1	19	89
3	99	startjo01	1871	1	NY2	33	161
4	102	suttoez01	1871	1	CL1	29	128
5	106	whitede01	1871	1	CL1	29	146
6	113	yorkto01	1871	1	TRO	29	145
7	121	ansonca01	1872	1	PH1	46	217
8	143	burdoja01	1872	1	BR2	37	174
9	167	forceda01	1872	1	TRO	25	130
10	168	forceda01	1872	2	BL1	19	95
11	186	hinespa01	1872	1	WS4	11	49
12	209	mathebo01	1872	1	BL1	50	223
13	226	nelsoca01	1872	1	TRO	4	20
14	227	nelsoca01	1872	2	BR1	18	76
15	229	orourji01	1872	1	MID	23	101
16	249	startjo01	1872	1	NY2	55	282
17	252	suttoez01	1872	1	CL1	22	107
18	259	whitede01	1872	1	CL1	22	109

How it works...

Pandas is a well-developed and tested suite of tools that provide a wide assortment of functionality for Python users. Note that there are similar reading methods for the other languages in play for Jupyter. The `read_fwf` function is one of many. In our example, we only passed in the file location, widths, and column names. There are a number of additional optional parameters as well. Of the other parameters, I can imagine using a `zip` parameter (for reading a zipped text file while it remains in the `.zip` file), whether to skip a number of rows at the start of the file (I think many flat files reserve this space for describing the file contents), and alternatively using column information with the positional start and end of each column rather than the widths of columns (especially if you want to skip over some fields in the file).

So, most of the work is done by `pandas`. We only have to correctly specify the widths and names for this to work as expected.

Reading text files

Text files, in contrast to those flat files, do not normally have column widths specified, nor do they have delimiters. The prototypical example would be programming logging files that are used by programmers to log the progress of their programs. The `log` files may have a consistent prefix to each record with a timestamp or such, but the rest of the record is completely up to the developer's needs.

Text files tend to be very large as well, easily running into many megabytes of storage.

An entirely new form of database has emerged for the storage and retrieval of text files, appropriately named text databases. Access to records in these databases is normally looking for strings that can be used to index the records. As before, `log` file entries normally have a consistent timestamp present, so you can order the results accordingly and file records occurring at particular times. You can just as easily look for any string in a text entry as well.

Getting ready

While it is interesting to actually load up a text into Jupyter, the follow-on work to determine word usage and meaning can be very enlightening. For our example, we need to locate a reasonable text source for access. Political speeches tend to be recorded verbatim via several sources. For our example, we can use President Trump's speech at a tax reform event recorded at `https://transcripts.factcheck.org/remarks-president-trump-tax-reform-event/`.

When reading a text file in R, the underlying component of the R libraries is expecting some basic constraints on the layout, particularly that the last record (carriage-return/linefeed-delimited set of text) is empty. That is not the case when accessing the URL mentioned just now. I then copied the text of the speech from the aforementioned URL and placed it in the local file `trump.txt` for further use, described as follows.

How to do it...

Using R, the script becomes:

```
#saved from
https://transcripts.factcheck.org/remarks-president-trump-tax-reform-event/
path <- "C:/Users/Dan/trump.txt"
text <- readLines(path, encoding="UTF-8")
```

It's more interesting to start processing the speech:

```
# create corpus
#install.packages("tm", repos='http://cran.us.r-project.org')
library(tm)
vs <- VectorSource(text)
elem <- getElem(stepNext(vs))
result <- readPlain(elem, "en", "idi")
txt <- Corpus(vs)
summary(txt)
```

This results in a corpus being created from the speech contents:

	Length	Class	Mode
1	2	PlainTextDocument	list
2	2	PlainTextDocument	list
3	2	PlainTextDocument	list
4	2	PlainTextDocument	list
5	2	PlainTextDocument	list

Some of the text processing that you can perform:

```
# convert to lower case
txtlc <- tm_map(txt, tolower)
inspect(txt[1])
inspect(txtlc[1])
```

You see that all the words have been changed to lowercase:

```
<<SimpleCorpus>>
Metadata:  corpus specific: 1, document level (indexed): 0
Content:  documents: 1

[1] For the second time in a month,<U+00A0>President Trump discussed his plans to change the tax cod
e. This is an annotated transcript of his remarks, which took place at the Indiana Farm Bureau Buildi
ng.<U+00A0>Click on the highlighted statements below to see a brief summary of statements that we and
others have fact-checked.<U+00A0>For more information, please read our story, <U+0093><U+0091>Death T
ax<U+0092> Talking Point Won<U+0092>t Die.<U+0094>
<<SimpleCorpus>>
Metadata:  corpus specific: 1, document level (indexed): 0
Content:  documents: 1

[1] for the second time in a month, president trump discussed his plans to change the tax code. this
is an annotated transcript of his remarks, which took place at the indiana farm bureau building. clic
k on the highlighted statements below to see a brief summary of statements that we and others have fa
ct-checked. for more information, please read our story, <U+0093><U+0091>death tax<U+0092> talking po
int won<U+0092>t die.<U+0094>
```

```
# some analysis of the speech
dtm <- DocumentTermMatrix(txt)
inspect(dtm)
```

```
<<DocumentTermMatrix (documents: 94, terms: 1048)>>
Non-/sparse entries: 3092/95420
Sparsity           : 97%
Maximal term length: 15
Weighting          : term frequency (tf)
Sample             :
    Terms
Docs and applause for have our tax that the will you
  10   2        1   1    2   2   1    1   7    0   0
  11  11        0   0    3   0   0    3   6    0   1
  45   7        1   3    3   0   3    4   8    0   1
  47   2        2   1    0   0   2    4   2    0   0
  51   4        1   2    1   2   0    1   1    0   1
  64   4        2   1    0   1   0    1   5    2   0
  67   2        1   1    2   0   0    2   3    1   3
  73   5        1   3    0   2   1    0   4    0   0
  80   5        1   0    3   0   3    0   6    2   2
  9    5        0   0    3   2   0    4   4    0   1
```

```
findAssocs(dtm, "tax", 0.15)
```

```
$tax =
       the  0.44
      cuts  0.43
       pay  0.37
    system  0.32
     lower  0.3
significant 0.3
    breaks  0.3
     farms  0.3
competitors 0.3
  numerous  0.3
     death  0.29
tremendous  0.29
     small  0.29
   because  0.27
    reform  0.27
 calculate  0.27
```

How it works...

We took one of the speeches by Trump and performed some text processing on the speech. Then we started some analysis of the speech content.

The first step in text processing is to transform the text into a corpus or a set of structured text pieces that can be easily manipulated by the libraries. The preceding display continues on for some length.

Once we have a corpus, we can perform a number of transformations. Some of the transformations available are:

- **Converting to lowercase (which makes comparisons easier)**: This is shown in the preceding coding
- **Removing punctuation**: This eliminates extraneous information from the corpus
- **Removing numbers**: Again, this is normally not of interest for text processing
- **Removing words**: The typical stop words are the target (the, and, of, and so on)
- **Removing whitespace**: Extra lines or spacing are ignored
- Converting to word stems (then we are able to compare stems versus uses)

One of the more interesting things to do (once these transformations have been made) is to create a document matrix of the results. A document matrix gives you details of frequency and adjacency. For this example, I selected the word **tax** and was interested in words that are normally adjacent to this word. The system found cuts, system, significant, and breaks—Trump really wants to lower taxes!

4
Visualizing Your Analytics

In this chapter, we will cover the following recipes:

- Generating a line graph using Python
- Generating a histogram using Python
- Generating a density map using Python
- Plotting 3D data using Python
- Presenting a user-interactive graphic using Python
- Visualizing with R
- Generating a regression line of data using R
- Generating an R lowess line graph
- Producing a Scatter plot matrix using R
- Producing a bar chart using R
- Producing a word cloud using R
- Visualizing with Julia
- Drawing a Julia scatter diagram of iris data using Gadfly
- Drawing a Julia histogram using Gadfly
- Drawing a Julia line graph using the Winston package

Introduction

These are the recipes for visualizing your analytics in Python, R, and Julia. There are some similarities in the approaches taken for visualizations. However, the steps in one language compared to another are different.

Generating a line graph using Python

We will use a basic `plot()` to show how graphics work in Python to generate a line graph. Then, we will use several other libraries for other interesting visualizations available from Python.

For this example, we are using made-up data to determine the number of births that have the same name and producing a line plot of the data.

How to do it...

We can use this Python script:

```
import pandas
import matplotlib
%matplotlib inline

baby_name = ['Alice','Charles','Diane','Edward']
number_births = [96, 155, 66, 272]
dataset = list(zip(baby_name,number_births))
df = pandas.DataFrame(data = dataset, columns=['Name', 'Number'])
df['Number'].plot()
```

With the resulting plot as:

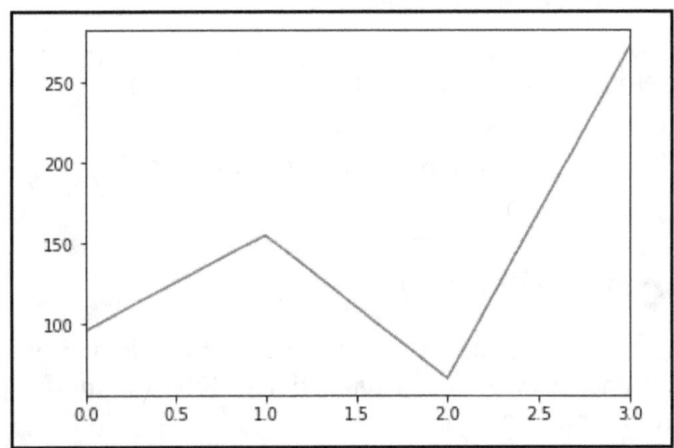

This is fictitious data, but it does show a good, clean graphic.

How it works...

pandas is the built-in Python library for dealing with a dataset. `matplotlib` is the Python library that will plot our data. We use the command `%matplotlib inline` to have the plot show up in our notebook. Otherwise, Python would generate the graphic in another screen or file.

We build up our dataset using `.zip` to combine the two columns. We convert the dataset into a data frame.

Now, we can call `plot` (since we have a data frame available). Note that there are extensive alterations you can make to the `plot` (such as title or x and y ranges); they are set using additional parameters to the command.

Generating a histogram using Python

In this example, we generate a histogram of random numbers. In this case, we are simulating rolling dice 1,000 times and recording the resultant face value.

How to do it...

We can use this Python script:

```
import pylab
import random

random.seed(113)

samples = 1000
dice = []
for i in range(samples):
 total = random.randint(1,6) + random.randint(1,6)
 dice.append(total)

pylab.hist(dice, bins= pylab.arange(1.5,12.6,1.0))
pylab.show()
```

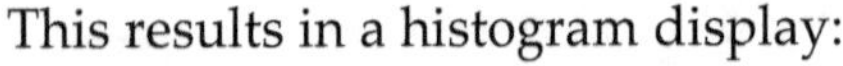

This results in a histogram display:

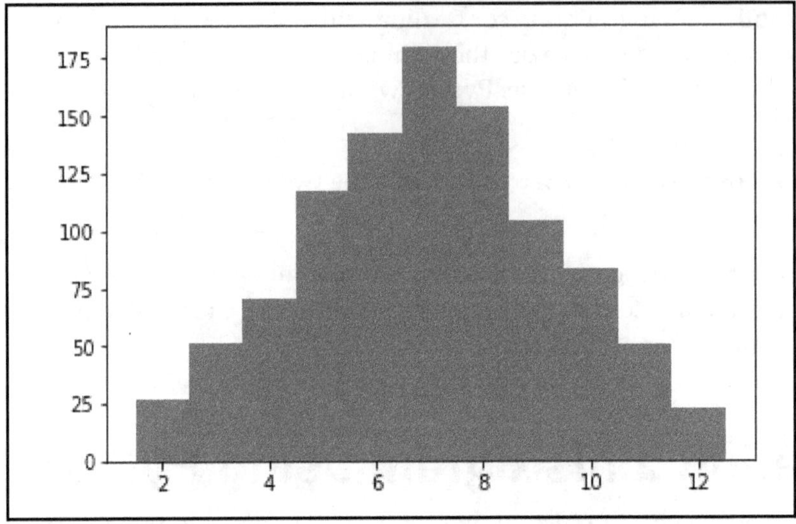

This is the graph showing almost exactly what we expected. I imagine that with a higher cycle count, we would have got closer to a pure pyramid peaking at **7**.

How it works...

For the histogram, we use the `pylab` library. We also use the random library to simulate the dice rolls.

We first set the random seed to a fixed value. This allows you to reproduce the results I have shown exactly.

Next, we simulate rolling the dice 1,000 times and record the results in an array. In this case, we are just recording the total of the two faces of the pair of dice.

Finally, we tell `pylab` to generate a histogram of the data. We are defining the size of the `bins` or collection points of the data for the display since we know exactly what the data is going to look like.

Also, we have to tell `pylab` to show the histogram. This allows `pylab` to keep a working copy of the graph in memory; it's for you to make further adjustments to the graphic, such as title or legend.

Generating a density map using Python

In this section, we generate a (human) density map of the United States, where each state is color coded based on its relative population density.

How to do it...

We can use the script:

```
%matplotlib inline

import matplotlib.pyplot as plt
from mpl_toolkits.basemap import Basemap
from matplotlib.patches import Polygon
import pandas as pd
import numpy as np
import matplotlib

# create the map
map = Basemap(llcrnrlon=-119,llcrnrlat=22,urcrnrlon=-64,urcrnrlat=49,
 projection='lcc',lat_1=33,lat_2=45,lon_0=-95)# load the shapefile, use the
name 'states'
# download from
https://github.com/matplotlib/basemap/tree/master/examples/st99_d00.dbf,shx
,shp
map.readshapefile('st99_d00', name='states', drawbounds=True)

# collect the state names from the shapefile attributes so we can
# look up the shape obect for a state by it's name
state_names = []
for shape_dict in map.states_info:
 state_names.append(shape_dict['NAME'])

ax = plt.gca() # get current axes instance

# load density data drawn from
# https://en.wikipedia.org/wiki/List_of_U.S._states_by_population_density
df = pd.read_csv('states.csv')

# determine the range of density values
max_density = -1.0
min_density = -1.0
for index, row in df.iterrows():
 d = row['density/mi2']
 density = float(d.replace(',' , ''))
```

```
 if (max_density==-1.0) or (max_density<density):
 max_density = density
 if (min_density==-1.0) or (min_density>density):
 min_density = density
print('max',max_density)
print('min',min_density)
range_density = max_density - min_density
print(range_density)

# we pick a color for the state density out of red spectrum
cmap = matplotlib.cm.get_cmap('Spectral')

# for each state get the color for it's density
for index, row in df.iterrows():
 state_name = row['State']
 d = row['density/mi2']
 density = float(d.replace(',' , ''))
 color = cmap((density - min_density)/range_density)
 seg = map.states[state_names.index(state_name)]
 poly = Polygon(seg, facecolor=color, edgecolor=color)
 ax.add_patch(poly)

plt.show()
```

The resulting display is as follows:

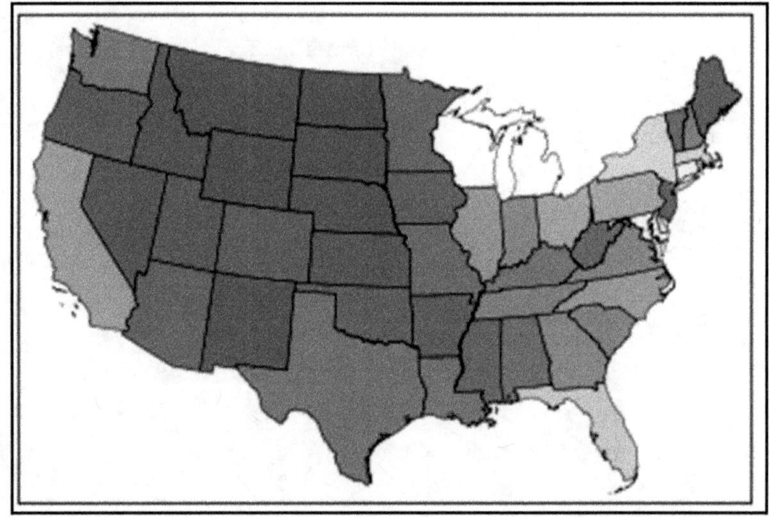

Most of the country is lightly populated. I was surprised that the northeast was even more populated than California, but this is density across the whole state, rather than Boston compared to Los Angeles, for example.

How it works...

First, we imported all of the packages needed to produce the graphic. Notice we are using sub-packages in a few instances. This is normal practice for Python coding.

The libraries used in this example are very particular to the operating system you are running and the version of Python you have installed. Visit the documentation online for `matplotlib` to understand the steps required for your environment.

We then created a (base) map using the state polygon image files downloaded from the internet. These are openly available for use. There are polygon sets for all countries and continents available.

We used the state population density factors from Wikipedia. We set them into a CSV file and then loaded them into our application. We then computed relative densities of the different states based on the data we have.

Now that we have the polygon (outline, position) of each state and its density color, we draw the map. Then, we use `show()` to actually display the map we have built up in memory onscreen.

Plotting 3D data using Python

In this example, we display 3D data. We take some automobile miles per gallon data and plot it out according to 3D weight, miles per gallon, and number of cylinders.

How to do it...

We use this script:

```
%matplotlib inline

# import tools we are using
import pandas as pd
import numpy as np
```

```
from mpl_toolkits.mplot3d import Axes3D
import matplotlib.pyplot as plt

# read in the car 'table' - not a csv, so we need
# to add in the column names
column_names = ['mpg', 'cylinders', 'displacement', 'horsepower', 'weight',
'acceleration', 'year', 'origin', 'name']
df =
pd.read_table('http://archive.ics.uci.edu/ml/machine-learning-databases/aut
o-mpg/auto-mpg.data', sep=r"\s+", index_col=0, header=None, names =
column_names)
print(df.head())

#start out plotting (uses a subplot as that can be 3d)
fig = plt.figure()
ax = fig.add_subplot(111, projection='3d')X# pull out the 3 columns that we
want
xs = []
ys = []
zs = []
for index, row in df.iterrows():
 xs.append(row['weight'])
 ys.append(index) #read_table uses first column as index
 zs.append(row['cylinders'])X# based on our dataset the extents of the axes
plt.xlim(min(xs), max(xs))
plt.ylim(min(ys), max(ys))
ax.set_zlim(min(zs), max(zs))

# standard scatter diagram (except it is 3d)
ax.scatter(xs, ys, zs)

ax.set_xlabel('Weight')
ax.set_ylabel('MPG')
ax.set_zlabel('Cylinders')

plt.show()
```

These are the intermediary results (head of the dataset):

```
      cylinders  displacement horsepower  weight  acceleration  year  origin  \
mpg
18.0          8         307.0       130.0  3504.0          12.0    70       1
15.0          8         350.0       165.0  3693.0          11.5    70       1
18.0          8         318.0       150.0  3436.0          11.0    70       1
16.0          8         304.0       150.0  3433.0          12.0    70       1
17.0          8         302.0       140.0  3449.0          10.5    70       1

                          name
mpg
18.0  chevrolet chevelle malibu
15.0          buick skylark 320
18.0         plymouth satellite
16.0              amc rebel sst
17.0                ford torino
```

These are obviously dated results. Many of these models are no longer in production.

The resulting graphic is displayed as follows:

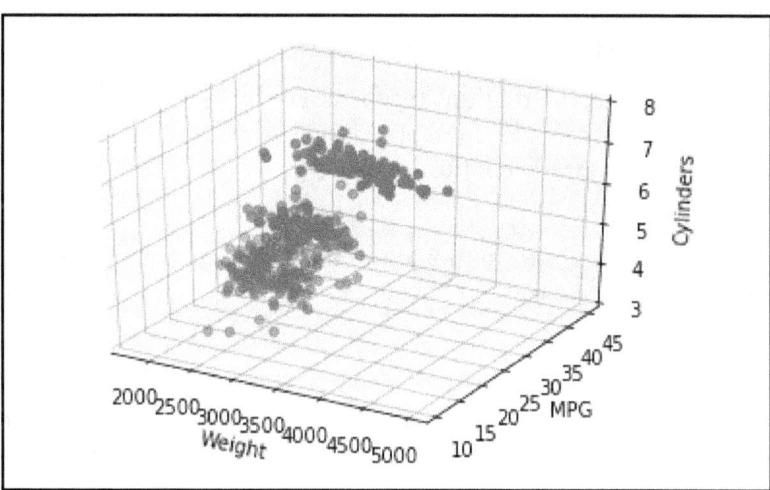

Interesting that the weight of the vehicle does not appear to have much effect on the `.mpg`! The number of cylinders, however, is a clear driver.

Not sure why the extent of the weight dimension went to 5,000 pounds. It does not look as though any vehicle weighs much more than 4,000 pounds.

How it works...

We load the libraries we are going to use. Again, it's important to set `matplotlib` to display the resulting graphic inline, that is, within our Jupyter script results.

We first load in the `.mpg` data from the CSV file. The file does not have column headers denoting which column is which, so we add those at the same time. The `print(head)` command results in the display of the first few rows of the dataset. This visually validates that our dataset is formatted correctly.

Next, we plot out each of the data points in the 3D format that we are concerned with. We also keep a track of the coordinate range limits (for later display).

Finally, we tell `matplotlib` that all of this data is a Scatter diagram and display it.

Present a user-interactive graphic using Python

In this section, we use another Python library, `bokeh`, to display a chart where the user can adjust parameters of the graphic for different results.

The installation instructions for the `bokeh` library are very complex. Again, they're specific to the operating system and version of Python you are using in your installation.

We are presenting online voter information, with the data points showing, for each user ID, how many votes they received for some post they made.

How to do it...

We can use this script:

```
from bokeh.io import output_notebook, show
from bokeh.layouts import widgetbox
from bokeh.models.widgets import TextInput
from bokeh.models import WidgetBox
import numpy as np
import pandas as pd
from bokeh.plotting import figure, show
```

```
from bokeh.layouts import layout

output_notebook()

# load the vote counts
from_counts = np.load("from_counts.npy")

# convert array to a dataframe (Histogram requires a dataframe)
df = pd.DataFrame({'Votes':from_counts})
#print(df.head())

p = figure(plot_height=200,plot_width=600, title="How Many Votes Made by
Users")
p.vbar(x=range(0,6110), width=0.5, bottom=0,
       top=df.Votes, color="firebrick")

button = Button(label="Foo", button_type="success")
text = TextInput(title="title", value='A Text Box')
widgets = WidgetBox(button, text)
l = layout([p,widgets])

show(l)
```

This results in this interactive graphic:

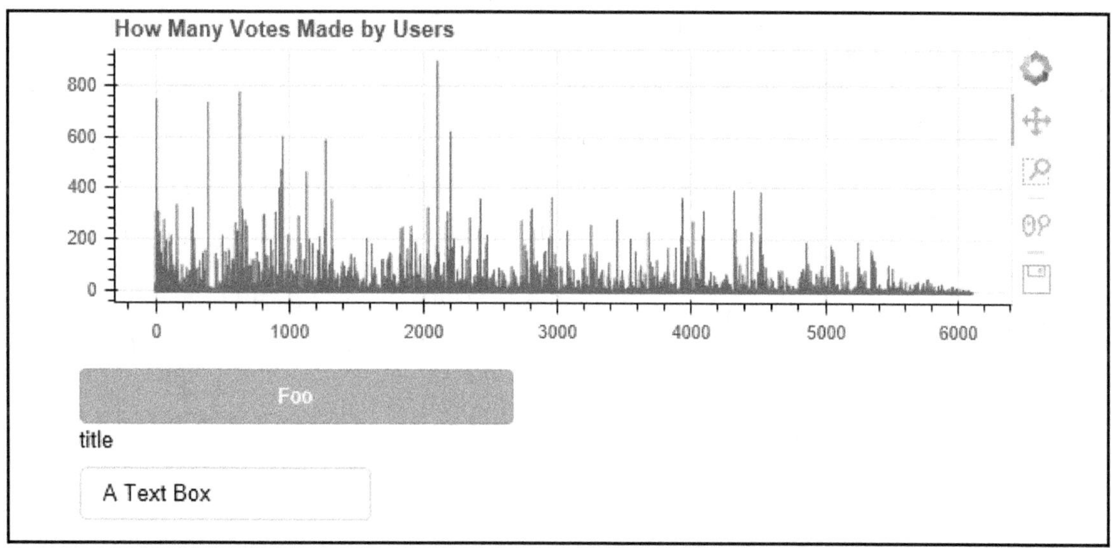

We find several interactive features present:

- Along the right-hand side of the graph are some standard buttons that work with any `bokeh` interactive graphic:
    - At the top is a graphic link to the bokeh site
    - Then, a cross-hair for repositioning the graphic on the page
    - Then, a magnifying glass for zooming into the graphic
    - A wheel zoom
    - And a way to save the graphic to a file
- The following is the graphic of the widgets that we added:
    - A button
    - A textbox for data entry with a title

How it works...

We are using many `bokeh` libraries. The most important for this example is the widgets set.

Since we are running this in a notebook, we direct the output to the Notebook with `output_notebook()`.

The next few lines are fairly boilerplate for creating a graphic of interest.

Then, we create the button and the text field. Both are added to a widgets object. Then, the widgets object and the graphic are placed into a `bokeh` layout object. There are several schemes available for layouts.

Finally, a show, passing the layout to the show routine.

You can also add handlers for dealing with the user clicking on a button or changing a value in a field to update your graphic dynamically. The handlers would be standard Python functions, `def method(): ...`, where the method is passed to the layout call.

Visualizing with R

There are several visualization mechanisms available in R.

- Produce a R Scatter plot

In this example, we produce a scatter plot using the standard R `plot()` function. Built into the plot function, we can chart the relationship between the `x` and `y` values as well.

How to do it...

We can use this script:

```
# load the iris dataset
data <-
read.csv("http://archive.ics.uci.edu/ml/machine-learning-databases/iris/iri
s.data")

#Let us also clean up the data so as to be more readable
colnames(data) <- c("sepal_length", "sepal_width", "petal_length",
"petal_width", "species")

# make sure the data is as expected
summary(data)
```

```
 sepal_length    sepal_width     petal_length    petal_width
 Min.   :4.300   Min.   :2.000   Min.   :1.000   Min.   :0.100
 1st Qu.:5.100   1st Qu.:2.800   1st Qu.:1.600   1st Qu.:0.300
 Median :5.800   Median :3.000   Median :4.400   Median :1.300
 Mean   :5.848   Mean   :3.051   Mean   :3.774   Mean   :1.205
 3rd Qu.:6.400   3rd Qu.:3.300   3rd Qu.:5.100   3rd Qu.:1.800
 Max.   :7.900   Max.   :4.400   Max.   :6.900   Max.   :2.500
            species
 Iris-setosa    :49
 Iris-versicolor:50
 Iris-virginica :50
```

Produce the Scatter plot:

```
plot(data$sepal_length, data$petal_length)
```

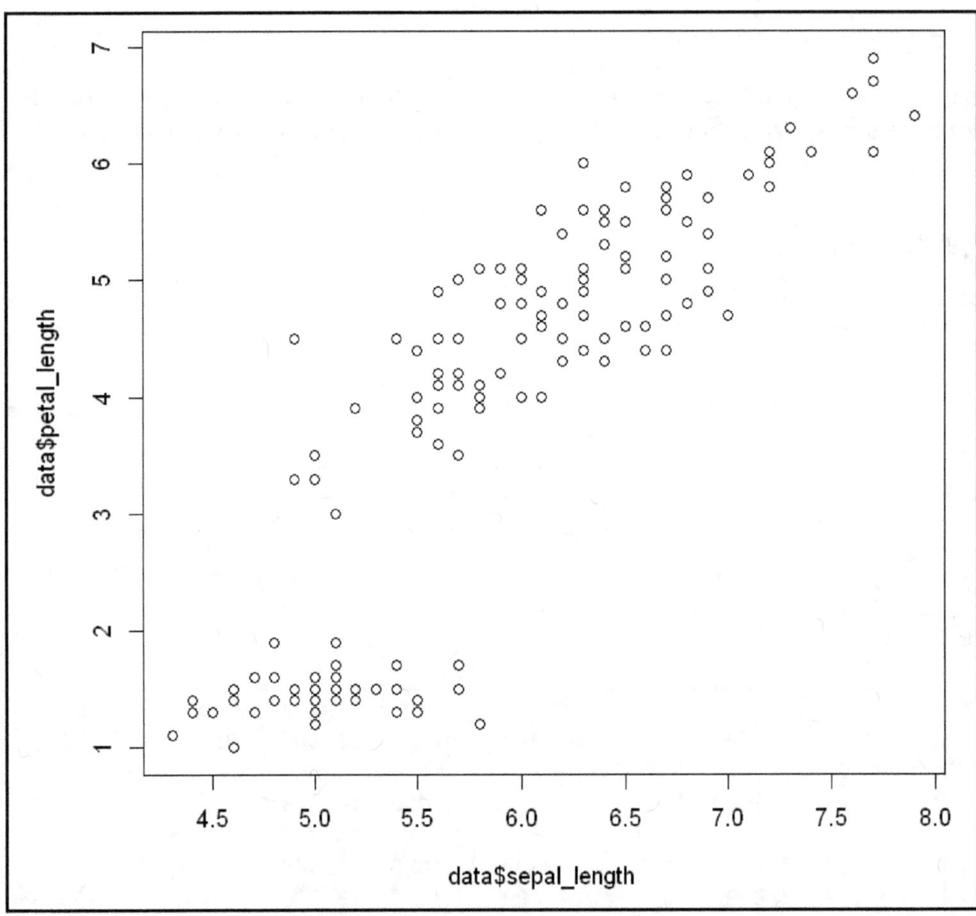

And produce the following visualizations of the relationships between the values. This plot is a stepwise look at how changing one value appears, to see the effect on the other:

```
plot(data$sepal_length, data$petal_length, type="s"
```

The output is as follows:

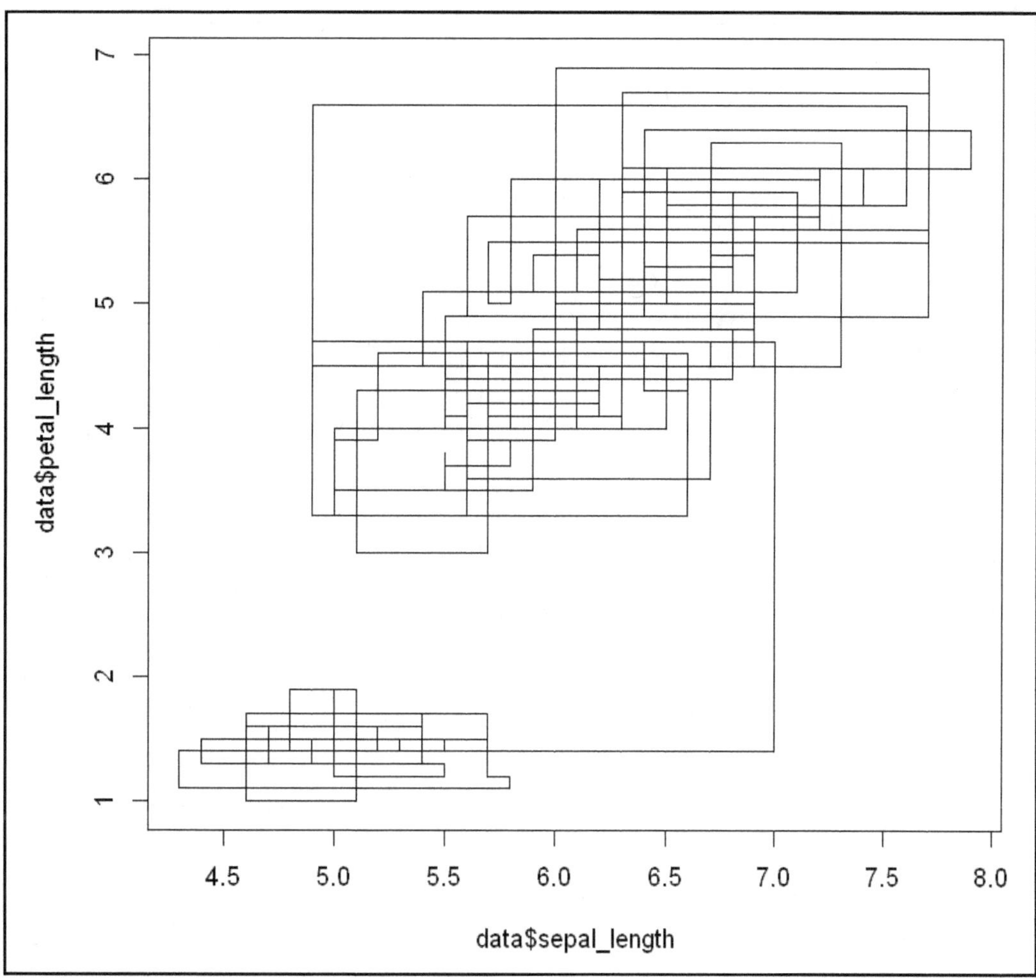

And we look at a histogram of the same data as is:

```
plot(data$sepal_length, data$petal_length, type="h")
```

The output is as follows:

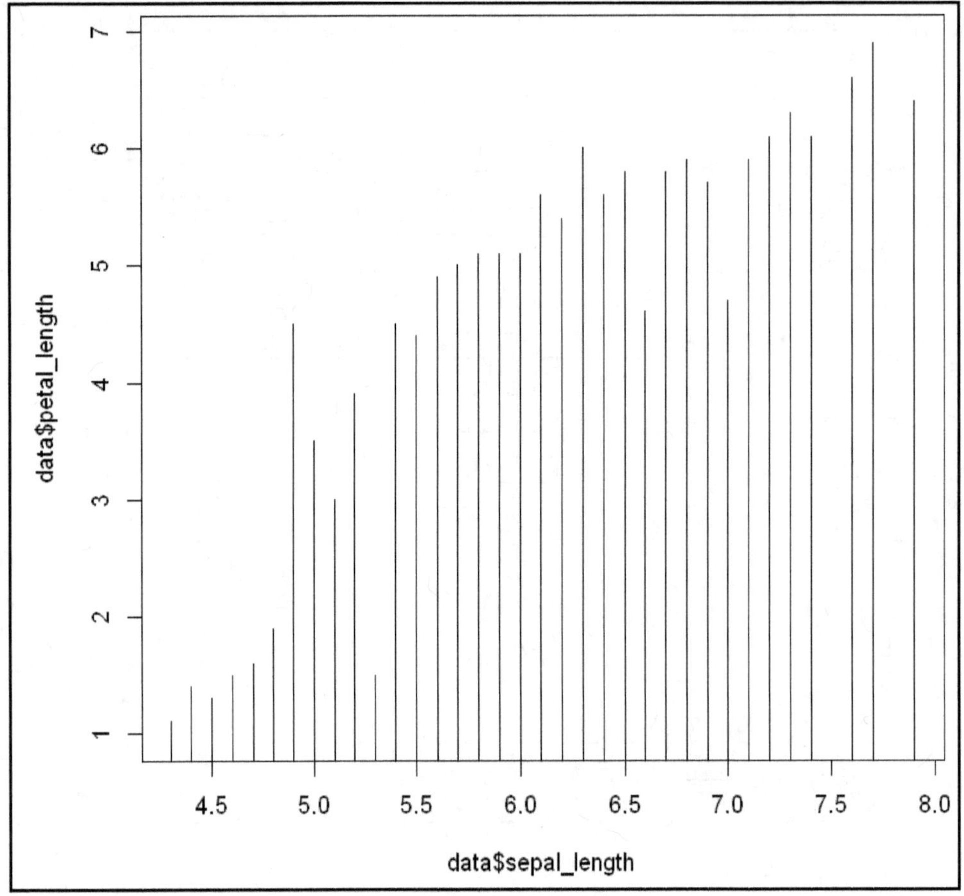

How it works...

We are visualizing the iris dataset, specifically looking for a relationship between petal length and sepal length.

We load the dataset and apply column names. We produce a summary to verify the data.

Then, we call upon the `plot()` command to produce a Scatter plot, a stepwise relationship plot between the two variables, and a histogram of the data points.

I think the stepwise plot is the most interesting as you can still see tight areas where changes keep the affected values in a small range.

Generate a regression line of data using R

In this example, we use the `abline` function to portray a regression line of our data.

How to do it...

We can use this script:

```
# load the iris dataset
data <-
read.csv("http://archive.ics.uci.edu/ml/machine-learning-databases/iris/iri
s.data")

#Let us also clean up the data so as to be more readable
colnames(data) <- c("sepal_length", "sepal_width", "petal_length",
"petal_width", "species")

# call plot first
plot(data$sepal_length, data$petal_length)

# abline adds to the plot
abline(lm(data$petal_length ~ sepal_length), col="red")
```

It results in a similar Scatter plot but with a regression line included:

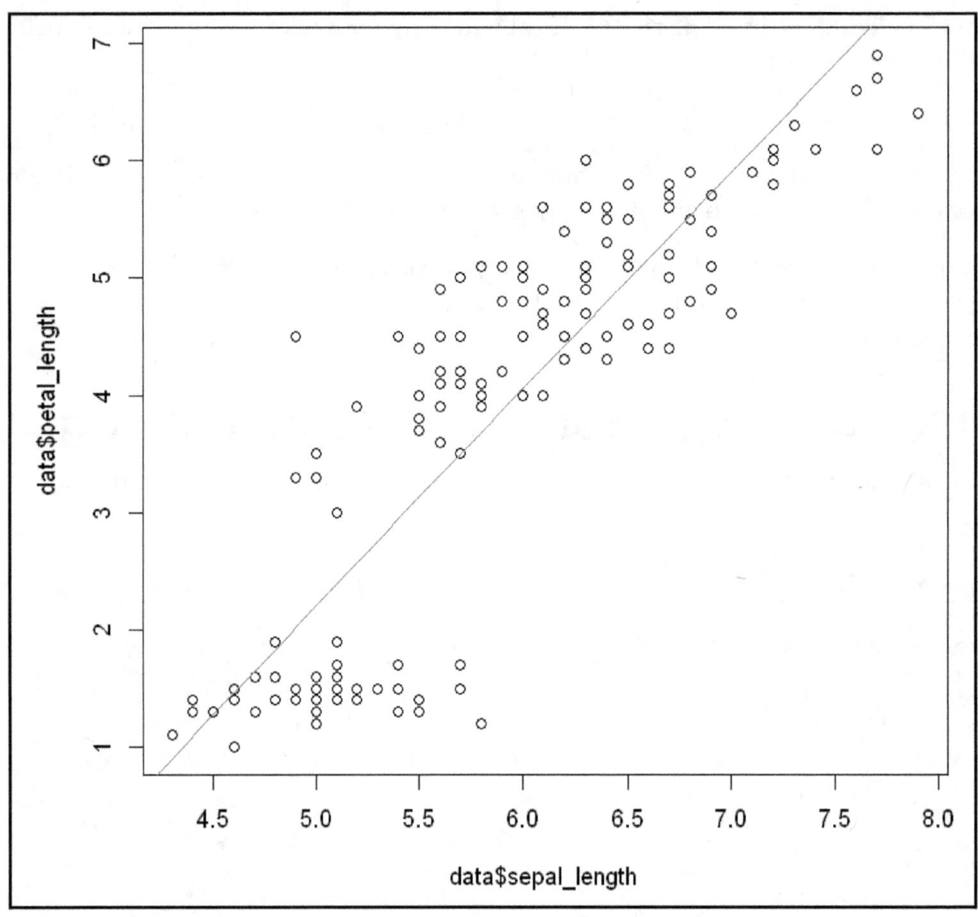

How it works...

We are using the same iris dataset as in the previous example.

We have seen how `plot` can produce a Scatter plot. The addition by `abline` is to calculate and draw out the regression line on top of the Scatter plot.

The regression does not appear to be a great fit as there are big chunks of data points far away from the line.

Generate an R lowess line graph

We can generate a `lowess` line on top of the Scatter diagram. The `lowess` line would likely show a better fit as smoothing is used to fit the line to the data.

How to do it...

We can use the same Scatter diagram as the basis and then call upon `lines` to add our `lowess` line:

```
# load the iris dataset
data <-
read.csv("http://archive.ics.uci.edu/ml/machine-learning-databases/iris/iri
s.data")

#Let us also clean up the data so as to be more readable
colnames(data) <- c("sepal_length", "sepal_width", "petal_length",
"petal_width", "species")

# call plot first
plot(data$sepal_length, data$petal_length)

# add the lowess line to the graph
lines(lowess(data$sepal_length, data$petal_length), col="blue")
```

Here is the resulting graph:

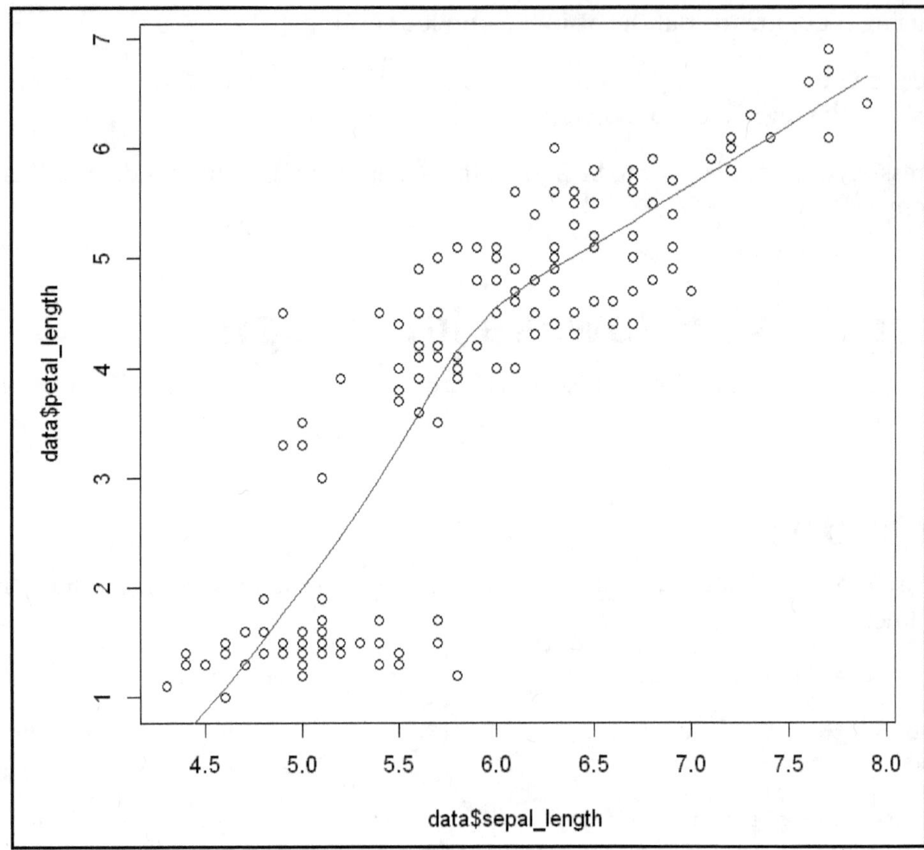

How it works...

Locally weighted scatterplot smoothing (**LOWESS**) is a useful mechanism when performing a regression to see a smoothed line drawn through our data. Once accomplished, you are likely to see relationships and possibly forecasts.

While the `lowess` line does fit the data better than simple regression, it does not appear to be an intuitive relationship as there is just a bump to attempt to line up better between the two groups of data points.

Producing a Scatter plot matrix using R

A Scatter plot matrix is a useful device to display a miniature Scatter plot of every variable in your dataset against every other variable. The resulting display gives you a quick scan to determine variables that may be related.

How to do it...

Use this script:

```
# load the iris dataset
data <-
read.csv("http://archive.ics.uci.edu/ml/machine-learning-databases/iris/iri
s.data")

#Let us also clean up the data so as to be more readable
colnames(data) <- c("sepal_length", "sepal_width", "petal_length",
"petal_width", "species")

pairs(data)
```

This produces this graphic:

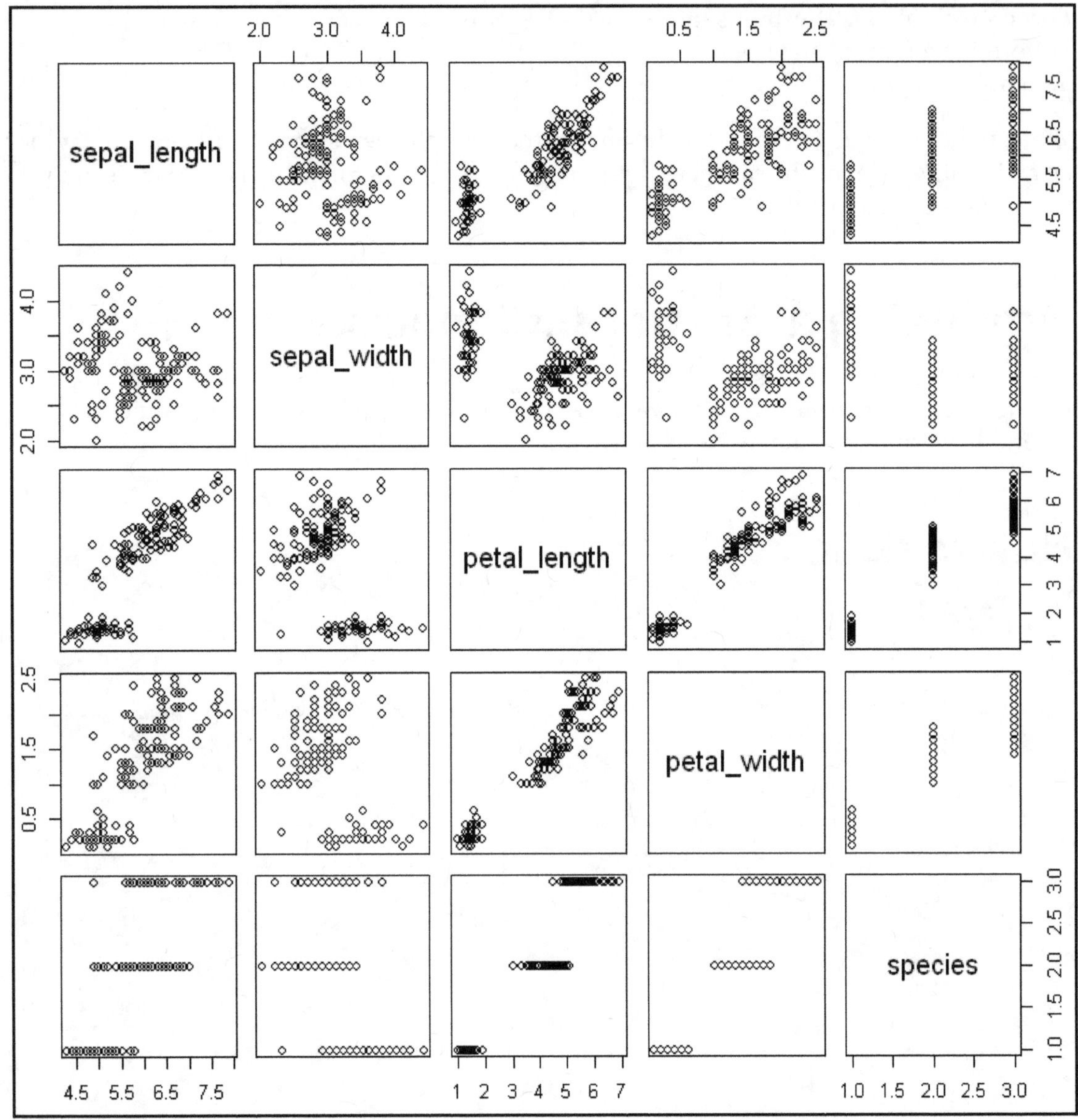

The pairs graphic shows petal width and petal length as related (fairly good straight lines of the plot points), and little relationship between sepal length and sepal width.

How it works...

The `pairs` function draws upon the underlying plot to walk through all `pairs` of data points in the dataset and produce a Scatter plot. I have used this many times to get a quick handle on which variables may be of interest to investigate further.

Producing a bar chart using R

There are several bar chart tools available from R. We will use the `barplot` function in this example.

How to do it...

We can use this script:

```
# we are using the haireyecolor data from the MASS library
library(MASS)
summary(HairEyeColor)
```

```
Number of cases in table: 592
Number of factors: 3
Test for independence of all factors:
        Chisq = 164.92, df = 24, p-value = 5.321e-23
        Chi-squared approximation may be incorrect
```

Excellent `p-value`, so we should have good data to work with!

```
# display the data
HairEyeColor
```

```
, , Sex = Male

       Eye
Hair    Brown Blue Hazel Green
  Black    32   11    10     3
  Brown    53   50    25    15
  Red      10   10     7     7
  Blond     3   30     5     8

, , Sex = Female

       Eye
Hair    Brown Blue Hazel Green
  Black    36    9     5     2
  Brown    66   34    29    14
  Red      16    7     7     7
  Blond     4   64     5     8
```

I hadn't thought about sex being a determinant. We will combine all of the data into one set:

```
# build a table of the information
counts <- table(HairEyeColor)
# produce the bar chart
barplot(counts)
```

That produces this result:

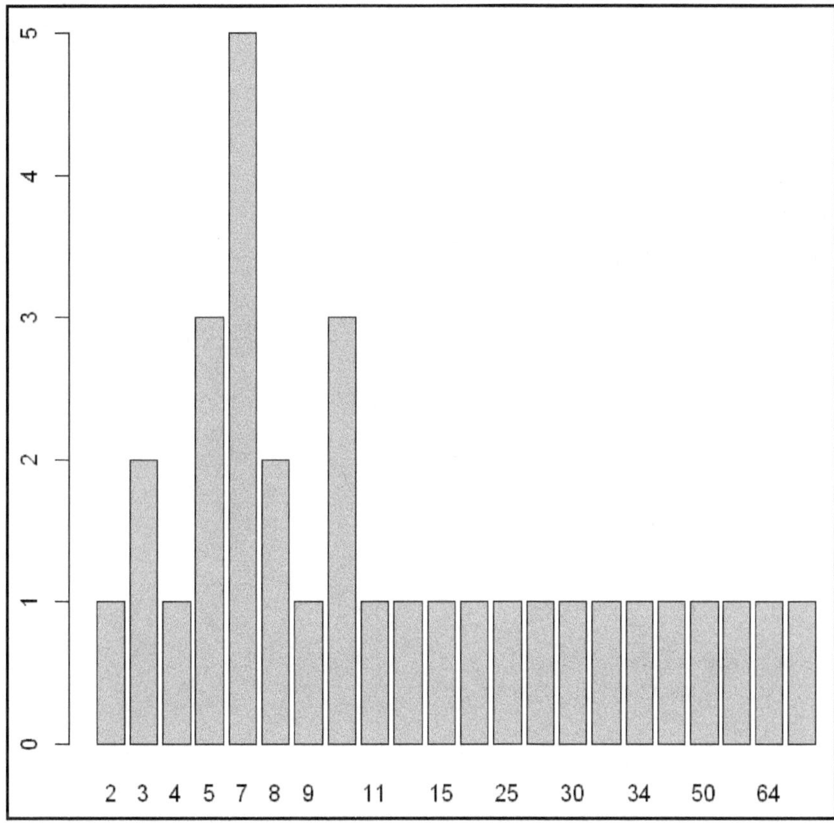

Interesting, that there are many cases with high coincidence (the 34s, 50s, and 64s) and there are many with low numbers (most under 10).

How it works...

We are displaying the relationship, if any, between eye color and hair color. The data is organized in that fashion already.

The `barplot` function takes the R table and maps out the appropriate bar chart.

Producing a word cloud using R

While many of the visualizations portray numeric data, we can also produce textual visualizations. In this case, we will produce a word cloud from data on a recent speech by president Trump.

How to do it...

We can use the following script:

```
library(tm)
#install.packages('wordcloud', repos='http://cran.us.r-project.org')
library(wordcloud)

#extracted from
https://www.lifesitenews.com/news/jesus-birth-changed-the-course-of-human-h
istory-trumps-extraordinary-2017-c
page <- readLines("trump-speech.txt")

# produce corpus of text
corpus <- Corpus(VectorSource(page))

# convert to lower case
corpus <- tm_map(corpus, tolower)
# remove punctuation
corpus <- tm_map(corpus, removePunctuation)
# remove numbers
corpus <- tm_map(corpus, removeNumbers)
# remove stop words
corpus <- tm_map(corpus, removeWords, stopwords("English"))

# reconfigure corpus as text document
#corpus <- tm_map(corpus, PlainTextDocument)
# create document term matrix from corpus
dtm <- TermDocumentMatrix(corpus)
# convert to a standard R matrix
m = as.matrix(dtm)
# sort highest usage
v = sort(rowSums(m), decreasing=TRUE)

wordcloud(names(v), v, min.freq=20)
```

It produces this word cloud:

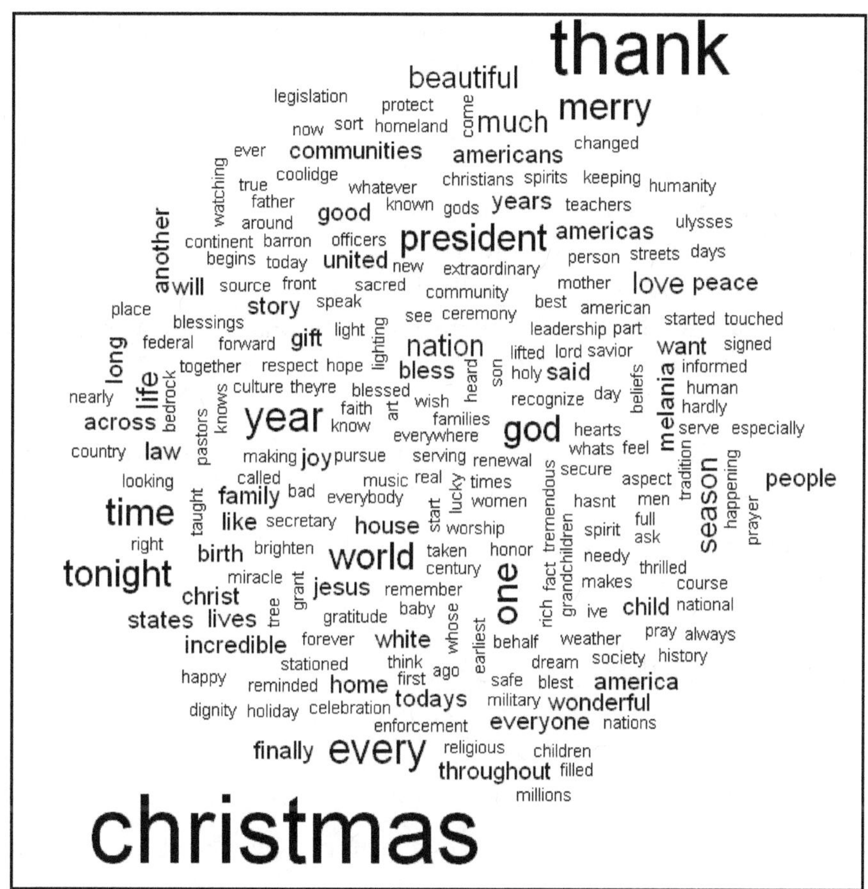

Although the website was putting down Trump for some parts of this speech, the word cloud looks very positive and in the seasonal spirit.

How it works...

There are several basic text processing techniques in use here. First, we build a corpus of the text. A corpus is a collection of text streams, typically paragraphs or pages of a book.

We then clean up the corpus in several steps:

- **Convert all of the text to lowercase**: This facilitates indexing of strings in the text without any concerns about capitalization.
- **Remove punctuation**: Punctuation is not of interest.
- **Remove numbers**: Again, we are looking for themes in the page.
- **Remove stop words**: Remove all the miscellaneous words, such as the, and, and then. I'm not sure if there is a stop words set to exclude all the HTML tags present on web pages.

We cannot produce a document matrix from the corpus. This produces a word index of usage throughout the page.

Finally, we take the matrix and produce a word cloud.

Visualizing with Julia

Julia is a programming language specifically built for numerical computing. There are several features that make it a great fit for use as a Jupyter scripting language. We will use several of the available packages for visualization.

Of special note is that Julia has direct access to most R packages, so those can be used as well.

A word of caution: I could not produce most Julia visualizations on a Windows PC. For this section, I used a Mac, and even then I had to try adding packages several times before things started to work.

Getting ready

Before using Julia scripts, you should add some standard packages and update all packages to the current levels. You can do that with these commands directly in the Julia console rather than in a Notebook:

I would recommend that you add a package by closing the Notebook, opening a Julia console, adding the package, reopening the Notebook, and then using the new package.

```
Pkg.add("DataFrames")
Pkg.add("RDatasets")
Pkg.add("Gadfly")
Pkg.update()
```

The packages will take some time to download and install. The process will produce voluminous output in Jupyter, as shown in the following display:

```
Pkg.update()

INFO: Cloning cache of AxisAlgorithms from https://github.com/timholy/AxisAlgorithms.jl.git
INFO: Cloning cache of Calculus from https://github.com/johnmyleswhite/Calculus.jl.git
INFO: Cloning cache of CommonSubexpressions from https://github.com/rdeits/CommonSubexpressions.jl.git
INFO: Cloning cache of Compose from https://github.com/GiovineItalia/Compose.jl.git
INFO: Cloning cache of CoupledFields from https://github.com/Mattriks/CoupledFields.jl.git
INFO: Cloning cache of DiffResults from https://github.com/JuliaDiff/DiffResults.jl.git
INFO: Cloning cache of DiffRules from https://github.com/JuliaDiff/DiffRules.jl.git
```

You may be better off running this update script directly into a Julia console window.

- Make a Julia Scatter plot

Here, we use a Scatter plot of random data points.

How to do it...

We can use this script:

```
#Pkg.add("Plots")
#Pkg.add("PyPlot")
using Plots
plotly()
srand(113)
plot(rand(5,5),title="My Random Plot")
```

It results in this output:

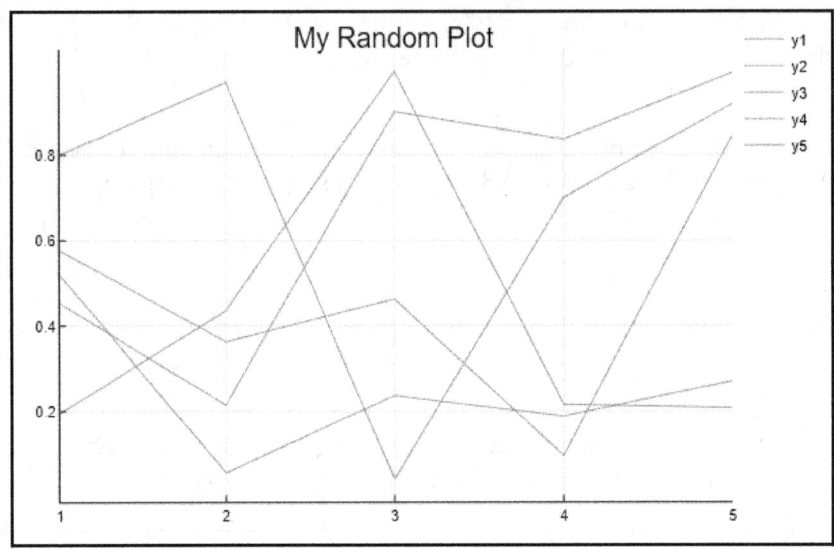

Note that we added the `plotly()` command. So, when we hover over the screen with the mouse, we see additional display fields available:

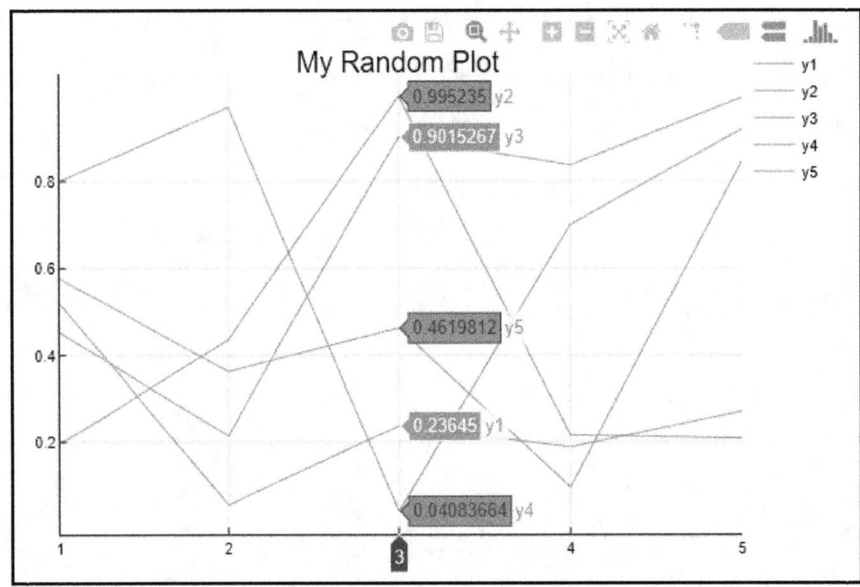

Where:

- The highlighted blocks are the values of the data points
- You can click on the camera icon to download the graphic file
- You can click on the diskette icon to save to the cloud
- The follow on icons can zoom, pan, zoom in, and zoom out

Drawing a Julia scatter diagram of Iris data using Gadfly

Gadfly is one of the major graphics packages available. In this example, we will be using the iris dataset as the source.

How to do it...

We can use this script:

```
using RDatasets, Dataframes, Gadfly
set_default_plot_size(5inch, 5inch/golden)
describe(dataset("datasets", "iris"))
plot(dataset("datasets", "iris"), x="SepalWidth", y="SepalLength",
color="Species")
```

We can see the described output:

```
In [2]: #Pkg.add("RDatasets")
        #Pkg.add("Dataframe")
        #Pkg.add("Gadfly")
        using RDatasets, DataFrames, Gadfly
        set_default_plot_size(5inch, 5inch/golden)
        describe(dataset("datasets","iris"))
        plot(dataset("datasets","iris"), x="SepalWidth", y="SepalLength",color="Species")

        SepalLength
        Summary Stats:
        Mean:           5.843333
        Minimum:        4.300000
        1st Quartile:   5.100000
        Median:         5.800000
        3rd Quartile:   6.400000
        Maximum:        7.900000
        Length:         150
        Type:           Float64
        Number Missing: 0
        % Missing:      0.000000
```

This is followed by the iris data plot:

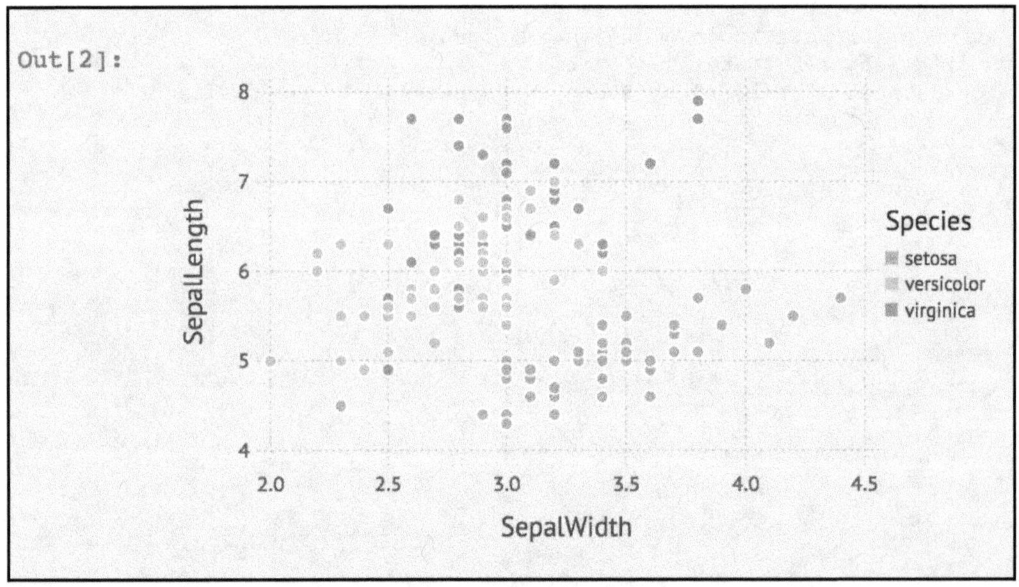

Drawing a Julia histogram using Gadfly

In this example, we produce a histogram using Gadfly.

How to do it...

We can use this small script:

```
using Gadfly
srand(111)
plot(x=randn(77), Geom.histogram(bincount=10))
```

That produces this plot:

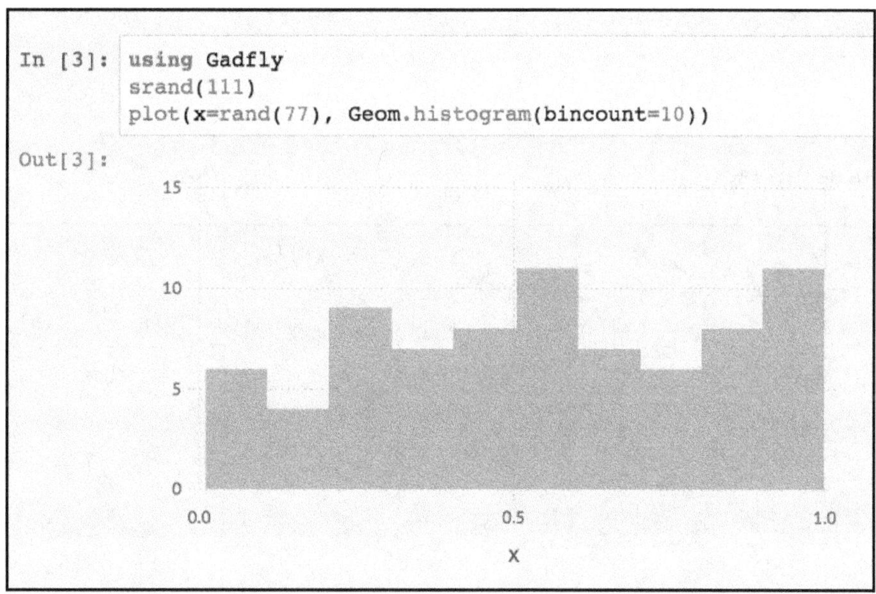

How it works...

We are using another part of Gadfly. In this case, we are selecting one of the geometric shapes of the histogram. Gadfly has quite a variety of shapes to choose from.

We tell Gadfly to break up the data into 10 bins for the histogram. For the example, we are generating 113 data points.

Drawing a Julia line graph using the Winston package

Another package for graphics in Julia is Winston. It has some of the capabilities of Gadfly and can produce similar plots.

How to do it...

We can use this script:

```
using Winston
srand(111)

#generate a plot
pl = plot(cumsum(rand(111) .- 0.5), "g", cumsum(rand(111) .- 0.5), "b")

display(pl)
```

That produces this plot:

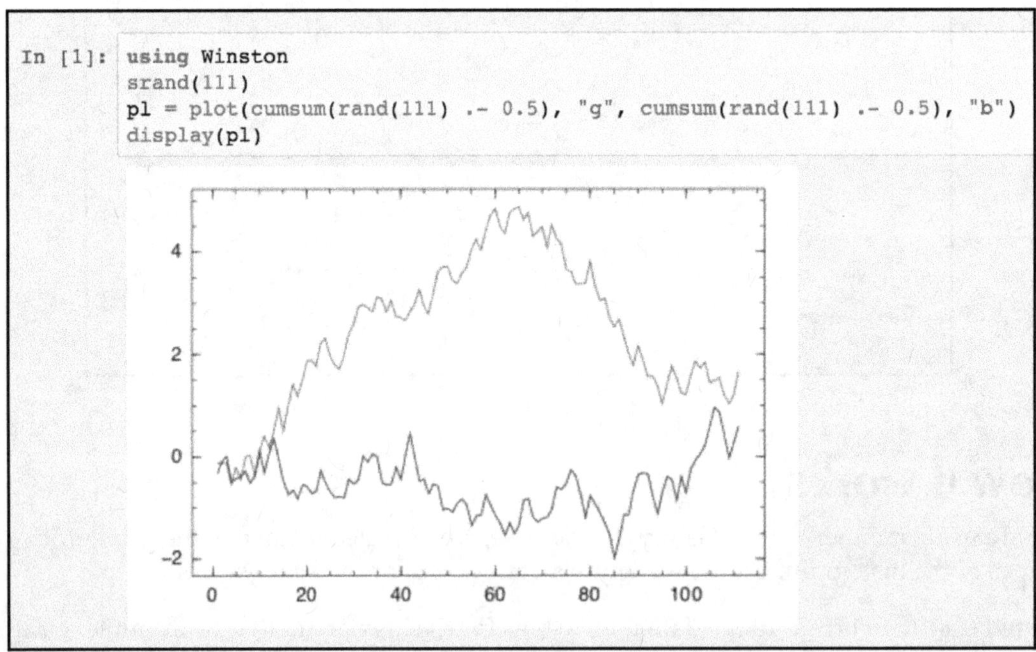

How it works...

We are plotting the cumulative sum of random points in a line graph.

Winston uses the idea of drawing to a plot and later actually displays the plot. This allows for adding legends, titles, and so on.

5
Working with Widgets

In this chapter, we will cover the following recipes:

- What are widgets?
- Using ipyleaflet widgets
- Using ipywidgets
- Using a cookie cutter widget
- Developing an OPENGL widget

Introduction

The Jupyter project has the specific objective of supplying a mechanism to reduce the gap between a user and their data. In this chapter, we will describe the wide range of possibilities of widgets in Jupyter. With these, we can include information for the user in a very good mood to show reporting of data in the same Jupiter tool. You will now make an interface like a human machine process; this will help you understand the basics of having programming software.

What are widgets?

Widgets are input devices that can be displayed in a Jupyter Notebook. The Notebook author controls the interaction with the input control and adjusts the Notebook display accordingly. By using widgets, the user has an input device or control that can be used to directly adjust data.

A widget can be of many types:

- Slider—the user is provided a control that can slide from one value to another
- Progress bar
- Input field for text and numeric values
- Toggle switch
- Checkbox
- Drop-down selection list
- Radio button
- Date picker
- Color picker
- A range of display-only devices, such as a valid data marker
- Adjustments to the Notebook, such as adding tabs to the display
- A catch-all, where you can produce your own custom widget

All input controls, where the user is typing or clicking, have a mechanism to provide feedback to the Notebook as to what action the user took; for example, if the user clicked on a button, a handler would be called in the Notebook. A handler is a language-specific set of code that is named. Calling a handler means invoking the set of steps associated with the handler.

Currently, the majority of widgets are available in Python notebooks. There are mechanisms available to pull them into other Notebook types, but that appears to be in flux. I expect that this will solidify over time.

Getting ready

There are some widget sets that are available directly. They are available in your Notebook like any other library that you need to include as per your requirement. Once included, the widget can be instantiated and called upon. When your Notebook is run, the widget will be activated and will be displayed according to how you set it up.

In this section, we will look at widget sets from `ipyleaflet`, `ipywidgets`, and interactive. I am sure the list of widget providers will grow over time as Jupyter's popularity increases. Also, if you do not find a widget that works in the manner you need, you can always produce your own custom widget using the building blocks provided by Jupyter.

How to do it...

In this example, we put a button control on our Notebook:

1. First, we reference the `widgets` library and the library to display the button:

```
import ipywidgets as widgets
from IPython.display import display
```

2. We create a button. This is like calling a library function, except that the function returns a `widget` object:

```
my_button = widgets.Button(description='Click My Button')
```

3. We need to display the button:

```
display(my_button)
```

4. When the user clicks, we want to print a message in the Notebook. We create the handler for the button clicks (we could've done any number of things, but in this example, we are just adding an output message):

```
def my_button_clicked(b):
    print("You clicked on My Button")
```

5. We have to tell the button where the handler is:

```
my_button.on_click(my_button_clicked)
```

6. That's the minimum needed. As with other library functions, we can call upon widgets and use default values for a number of settings.
   This will display on the page as follows:

```
In [16]: import ipywidgets as widgets
         from IPython.display import display

In [17]: my_button = widgets.Button(description='Click My Button')
         display(my_button)

         Click My Button

In [18]: def my_button_clicked(b):
             print("You clicked on My Button")

In [19]: my_button.on_click(my_button_clicked)
```

Note that the button is displayed inline with our text, `Click My Button`.

7. And when we click on the button, this will display:

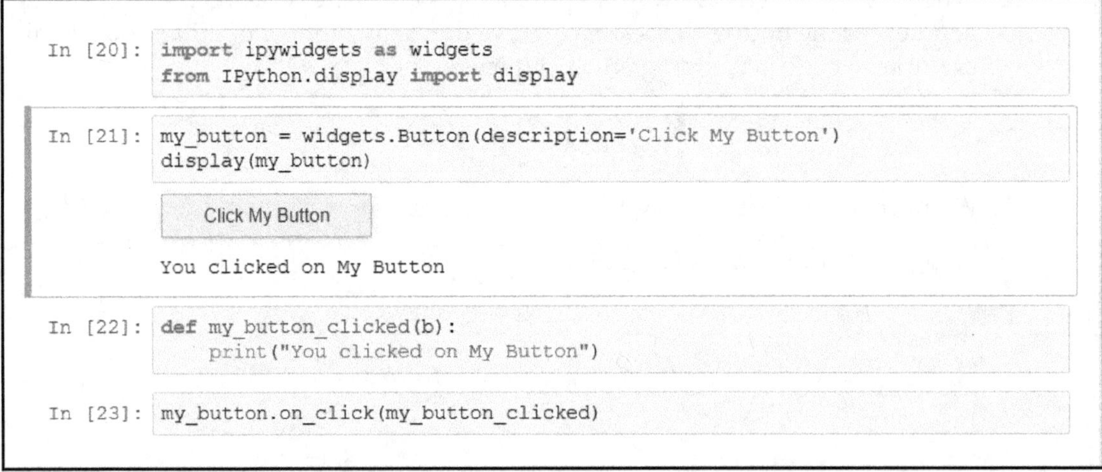
In [20]: import ipywidgets as widgets
from IPython.display import display
In [21]: my_button = widgets.Button(description='Click My Button')
display(my_button)
Click My Button
You clicked on My Button
In [22]: def my_button_clicked(b):
print("You clicked on My Button")
In [23]: my_button.on_click(my_button_clicked)

Note the additional display inline with our message, `You clicked on My Button`.

8. Clicking on the button repeatedly will add more copies of the message to the output area of the cell.

How it works...

Most of the coding here is standard Python Notebook behavior. There are a few new interactions with the system:

- The handler is registered with the underlying widget system. The system needs to know what code, if any, to invoke when an action occurs.
- When a corresponding action occurs, the system calls upon the cell where the handler is located to invoke the handler.
- In our case, the button handler displays a message. The default location for the message to be displayed is in the same cell as the button control. This means when the button was created, the underlying system recorded which cell it was in. The system then draws upon that cell location to output the handler.
- Finally, the handler adds to the appropriate cell output.

Using ipyleaflet widgets

`ipyleaflet` is described as a bridge for producing interactive maps in a Jupyter Notebook. This means we can put a map into a Notebook and allow the user to scroll around to a different point of view with this widget.

The documentation on the maps used is sparse. I have found a reasonable example in the following points. Finally, looking at the source code for the widget on GitHub, there are a few dozen maps visible that the widget knows about and which can be pulled in.

Getting ready

We can install the widget using a `conda` command:

```
conda install -c conda-forge ipyleaflet
```

`ipyleaflets` can be installed with `pip` as well.

Once completed, we can reference `ipyleaflet` in a Notebook.

How to do it...

We are using a detailed worldwide street map from `Esri`. The Notebook statements are:

```
from ipyleaflet import *
m = Map(zoom=4, basemap=basemaps.Esri.WorldStreetMap)
m
m.zoom
```

This generates the first image of the west coast of Africa. I navigated to the streets of Boston for the shot.

How it works...

The Basemap project appears to be expansive. There are many references to it from several map-producing organizations. Once we have a map for reference, the user control/widget then navigates over that map just as we would navigate over another data source.

Looking into the source code for the widget, we realize that the widget draws upon the interact widget as a basis. The interact widget produces events about what the user is doing, so the same events should still be triggered.

Using ipywidgets

`ipywidgets` is a set of widgets produced as part of the Jupyter project. As such, I would expect their use and number to increase with the project's popularity.

Getting ready

`ipywidgets` can also be installed with `conda` using:

```
conda install -c conda-forge ipywidgets
```

There are `pip` install commands available as well.

- Using an `ipywidget`

I picked the radio button widget as an example.

How to do it...

We can use this code:

```
import ipywidgets as widgets

widgets.RadioButtons(
 options=['red', 'green', 'blue'],
 description='Balloon color:',
 disabled=False
)
```

This displays as:

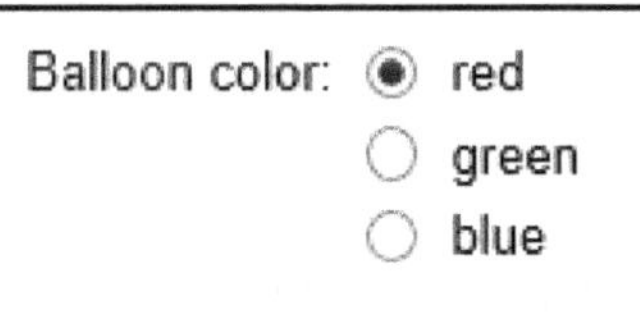

How it works...

All of the individual widgets work the same:

- Import the reference of the widget type you want to use
- Instantiate the widget using its parameters
- Optionally add handling to take a new value from the widget

In this example, we are using the Python convention of importing the entire library and calling it widgets. Then we use a specific widget type by referencing it via the dot notation. Each of the widget types has both common arguments and control-specific arguments to the constructor. The common arguments are elements such as description and disabled. The control-specific arguments are elements such as options for a radio button.

Using a widget container

A container is usually a box that groups controls/widgets together. You can imagine if you had a large form with many widgets; it would make it easier for the user if widgets are grouped into different containers like items.

How to do it...

We can use this script:

```
from ipywidgets import *
from IPython.display import display

slider = widgets.FloatSlider()
message = widgets.Text(value='Hello World')

container = widgets.Box(children=[slider, message])
container.layout.border = '1px black solid'

display(container)
```

This results in a display:

The container box instantiates like other widgets. The difference is that we pass in the list of contained widgets in its constructor. Once constructed, we can add different adornments, such as a border. Then, like other graphical elements, we display the container, which automatically draws its contained widgets as well.

Using an interactive widget

`interactive` is another set of widgets in the `ipywidget` library. They are specifically built to expect to call upon a handler when the value changes.

How to do it...

We can use this script:

```
def mycheckfunction(x):
    print(x)
    return x

interactive_checkbox = interactive(mycheckfunction, x=False)
interactive_checkbox
```

This results in this display:

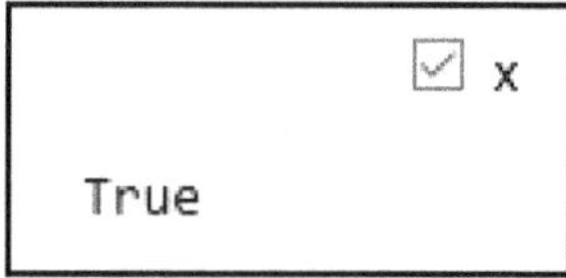

Here, as we click on the checkbox, the value of the box changes and the corresponding value is printed in the display.

How it works...

The constructor for the interactive widget has the first argument as the name of the handler to use when the value changes. The second argument is the default value. In this case, we have a checkbox, so the value is `False`. It could be `True` as well.

When you click on the box the value changes, triggering a call to the handler. The handler prints out the current value of the box.

Using an interactive text widget

Another interactive widget is a textbox. We using a text widget and gather changes as they occur in the box.

How to do it...

We can use this script:

```
def mytextfunction(x):
    print(x)
    return x

interactive_text = interactive(mytextfunction, x="Hello World")
interactive_text
```

It gives this display:

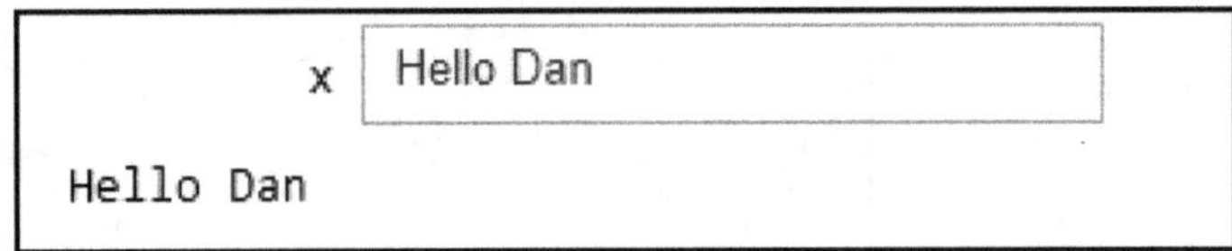

How it works...

Unexpectedly, the value changes on every keystroke you enter in the textbox, causing the printed display to mirror your typing.

Linking widgets together

We saw individual widget use earlier. We will now link widgets in the following examples.

How to do it...

We can link together two widgets using code like this:

```
import ipywidgets as widgets

floatTextBox = widgets.FloatText()
floatSlider = widgets.FloatSlider()
display(floatTextBox,floatSlider)

widgetLink = widgets.jslink((floatTextBox, 'value'), (floatSlider,
'value'))
```

It produces a display of both widgets linked together. If you move the slider, then the textbox value will be updated and vice versa:

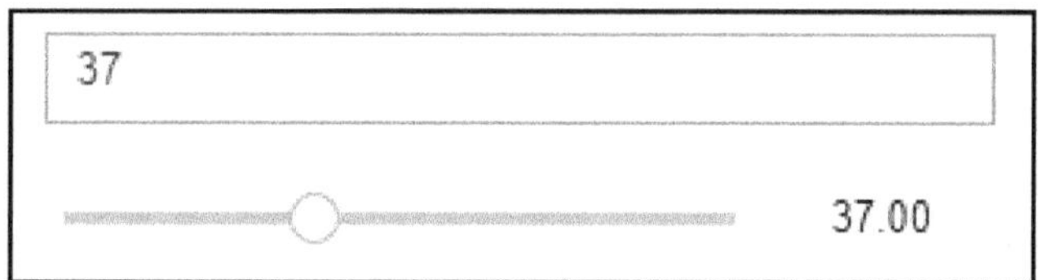

How it works...

We can link two widgets together using a call to `widgets.jslink`. Whenever one widget changes (in an attribute such as `value`), we can have another widget take that new value for itself and re-display it.

The key to this feature is the `js` in the method signature. Under the hood, we are using `javascript` event processing based on changes to the `value` of the objects. Of course, the actual display of the text value and moving the slider control is part of `ipywidgets`.

Another ipywidgets linking example

We can link one of the controls to a graphic display, which I think is much more interesting.

How to do it...

We can use the following code:

```
%matplotlib inline
from ipywidgets import interactive
import matplotlib.pyplot as plt
import numpy as np

def f(r):
 plt.axes()
 circle = plt.Circle((0, 0), radius=r, fc='y')
 plt.gca().add_patch(circle)
 plt.axis('scaled')
 plt.show()

interactive_plot = interactive(f, r=(0.0, 1.0))
output = interactive_plot.children[-1]
output.layout.height = '350px'
interactive_plot
```

The display looks like is:

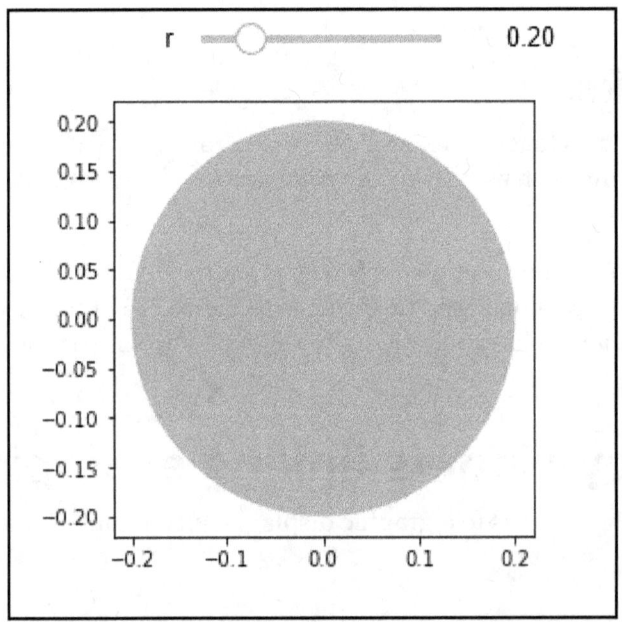

How it works...

Changing the position of the slide bar changes the value of the slide bar. The new value of the slide bar is used to repaint the circle image using the slide bar value as the radius of the circle.

Just as we saw in the previous linking example, the underlying code is attaching an event listener (the `f` function we defined just now) to the slide bar. When the value of the slide bar changes, it calls upon the event handler to deal with the value change. The handler redraws the circle graphic with the radius value supplied.

Using a cookie cutter widget

Cookie cutter is a project that provides a skeleton framework for a project—a project to make a project. In particular, you can generate the framework, skeleton, or starter files for creating your own widget.

Getting ready

You first need to install `cookiecutter`. We had used `conda` to install Jupyter, so we can use `conda` to install `cookiecutter` as follows:

```
conda install cookiecutter
```

You can also use `pip`.

Also, it is assumed that you will be producing your widget for consumption by the whole world. The current mechanism for doing this is to have the code for your widget stored in a GitHub repository for all to see.

`cookiecutter` does not work on Windows.

How to do it...

1. We first have to generate our skeleton widget by invoking `cookiecutter`:

```
cookiecutter https://github.com/jupyter/widget-cookiecutter.git
```

Here, we are running the `cookiecutter` code. It will automatically prompt for a number of settings regarding your widget, as follows:

```
author_name []: Dan Toomey
author_email []: dan@dantoomeysoftwarec.om
github_project_name []: DanToomeyWidget
github_organization_name []: Dan Toomey Software
python_package_name [DanToomeyWidget]:
npm_package_name [DanToomeyWidget]: DanToomeyWidget
npm_package_version [0.1.0]:
project_short_description [A Sample Widget]:
```

2. The values you enter will be inserted into the template code downloaded from the `cookiecutter` Git repository referenced. The code will then be generated into the appropriate directory, in this case, into the `DanToomeyWidget` directory.
3. When you open the project in the development environment tool IntelliJ, you will see this layout:

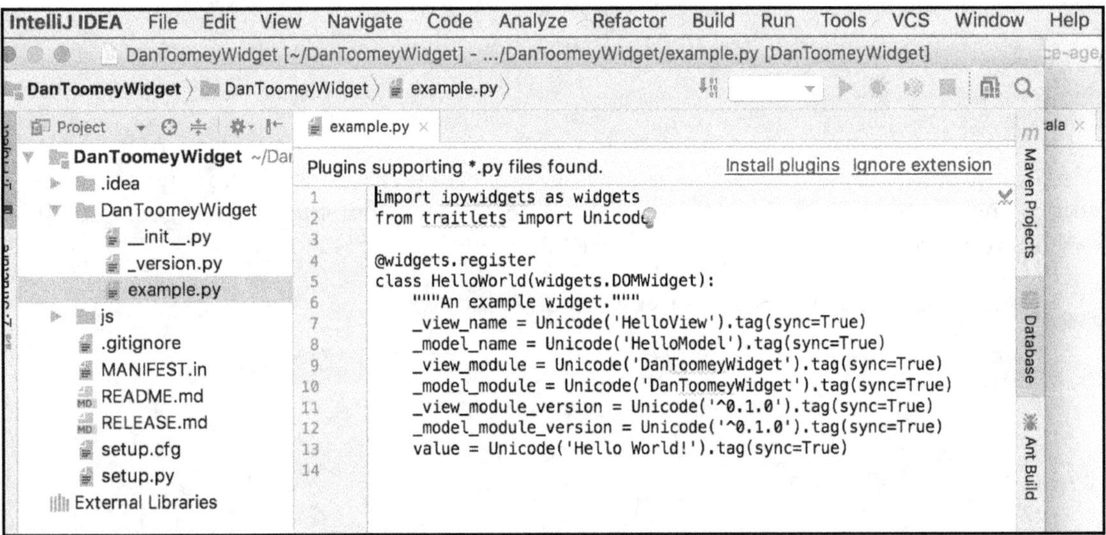

Most of the files are standard and you will not change them. The template provided assumes that `example.py` contains your project files. You can see the `@widgets.register` annotation; it will use this entry point to register with Jupyter.

The skeleton works without any change, but it must be built and registered first. The steps are as follows:

1. Build an `install` (locally):

```
python setup.py build
pip install -e
```

2. Register the widget with Jupyter using:

```
jupyter nbextension install --py --symlink --sys-prefix
DanToomeyWidget
jupyter nbextension enable --py --sys-prefix DanToomeyWidget
```

3. Try it out in a Notebook:

```
from DanToomeyWidget import example
hello_world = example.HelloWorld()
hello_world
```

You will receive the following result:

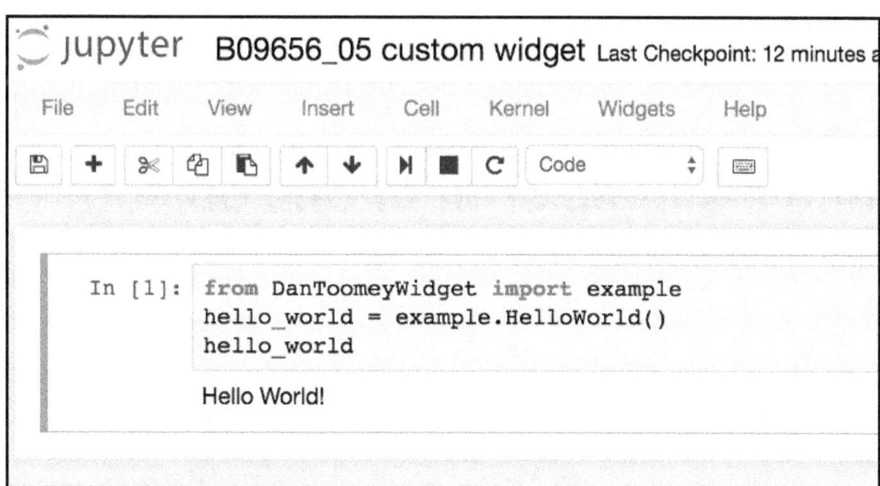

How it works...

With the skeleton framework installed, simply using the register annotation is all that we need to do to produce a widget that can be registered and used. Of course, any useful widget will have expansive functionality beyond this simple message.

Developing an OPENGL widget

A section of OPENGL, Rebound/WebGL, is available as a widget. Rebound can be used to portray objects in orbit under the effects of gravity.

Not the typical statistical subject, but it's useful in determining solutions in an area that has vast amounts of data to be analyzed. And more importantly, it shows how far you can go with a widget.

Getting ready

We first need to install `rebound` using `pip`:

```
pip install rebound
```

`rebound` does not work on Windows.

Creating a simple orbit of one object

We can have a single body in a standard orbit using default values.

How to do it...

If we use this script:

```
import rebound
sim = rebound.Simulation()
sim.add(m=1)
sim.add(a=1)
fig = rebound.OrbitPlot(sim)
fig
```

We have the resulting figure:

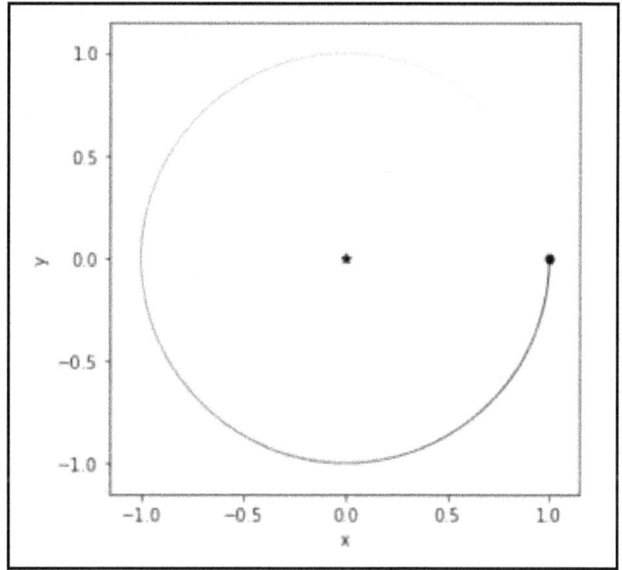

How it works...

Any instance of rebound starts with the `Simulation()` command.

`add(m=1)` adds a star in the center of the diagram. `add(a=1)` adds an object in orbit about `m`. In this case, many defaults take effect, resulting in this very standardized circular orbit.

Using a complex orbit of multiple objects

The simulation scenario allows for easily adding more objects with varied orbit patterns.

How to do it...

We can use a script like this:

```
import rebound

# setup simulation
sim = rebound.Simulation()
sim.getWidget()

# add star
sim.add(m=1)

# add ten 'planets'
for i in range(10):
 sim.add(m=1e-3, a=0.4+0.1*i, inc=0.03*i, omega=5.*i)

# center all particles
sim.move_to_com()

# advance the simulation
sim.integrate(500)

# get our final display on screen
fig = rebound.OrbitPlot(sim)
fig
```

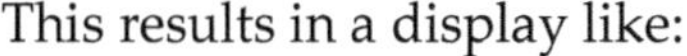

This results in a display like:

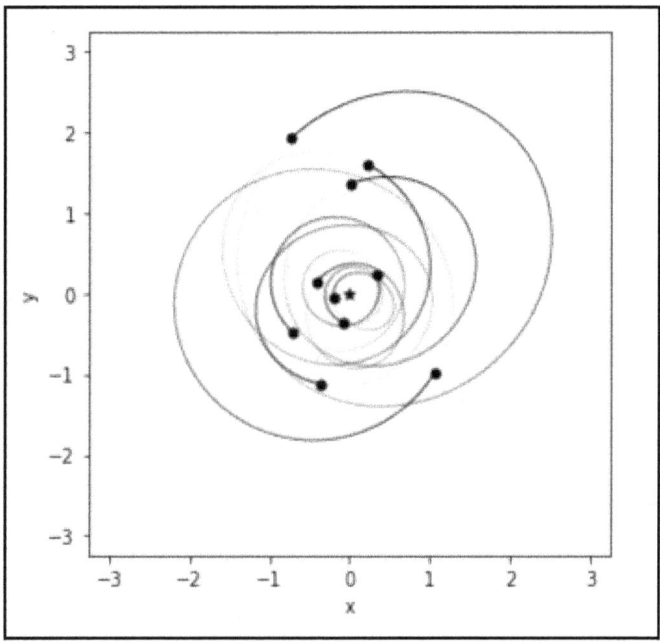

How it works...

Just as with the simpler case, we start a simulation. Then, in this case, we add a couple of objects. Each of the objects has a complex orbit about the star. We advance the clock by hundreds of cycles with `sim.integrate(500)` to gather a complete picture, and we display the results.

6
Jupyter Dashboards

In this chapter, we will cover the following recipes:

- What is Jupyter dashboards?
- Creating an R dashboard
- Creating a Python dashboard
- Creating a Julia dashboard
- Developing a JavaScript (Node.js) dashboard

Introduction

Jupyter dashboard is an extension for Jupyter that allows the Notebook developer to create a view of a Notebook in a specific layout without the reader working with the underlying Notebook script coding. There are two layouts:

- **Grid layout**: The screen is laid out in a grid, allowing you to arrange elements vertically and horizontally within the screen
- **Report layout**: Close to a standard Notebook, where elements are laid out vertically down the page

What is Jupyter dashboards?

In this recipe, we will learn how to install and enable Jupyter dashboards layout extension to your Notebook.

Getting ready

You first need to install the extension in your environment. You can use the `conda` command:

```
conda install jupyter_dashboards -c conda-forge
```

You can also use `pip` to install.

Assuming you have a set of items from a Notebook in mind, you first need to start Jupyter with the extension enabled. You enable the extension once from the command line (every time you start your computer) using the following command:

```
jupyter nbextension enable jupyter_dashboards --py --sys-prefix
```

You can then start your Notebook as usual.

How to do it...

When you start your Notebook, there is an icon gadget set at the top of the Notebook that you can work with:

If you hover over the middle icon you get a submenu:

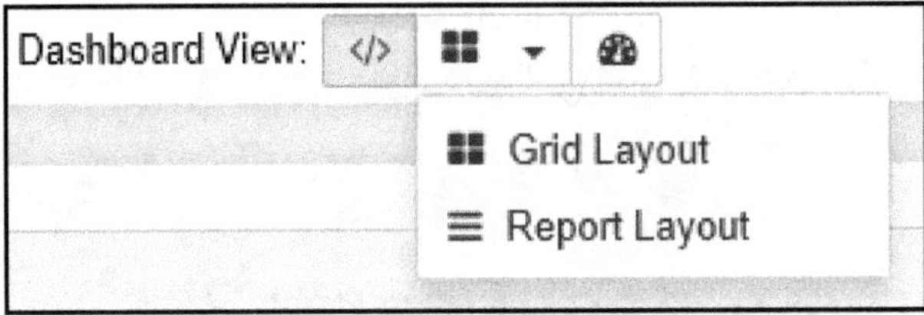

It has the corresponding **View** menu items:

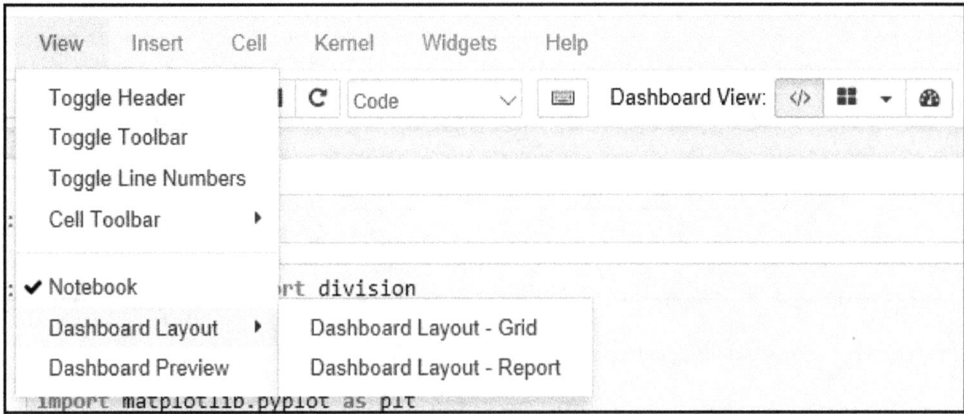

The icon gadget and menu items are:

- **Notebook**: Edit the code
- **Dashboard Layout**:
    - **Grid layout**: Size and position of the dashboard cells in a grid
    - **Report layout**: Size and position of the dashboard cells in a list
- **Dashboard Preview**: Preview the dashboard

Notebook edit view is the Notebook view that you have always used; cells are laid out top to bottom, with cell output interwoven as it occurs.

In either layout view, you can decide on the relative position and size of your items. You have the ability to:

- Move items by selecting and dragging the mouse to the desired position
- Resize items using the handles in the corners of each item
- Decide whether to display underlying code or not

In the layout view, the Notebook takes on a different appearance by providing these controls:

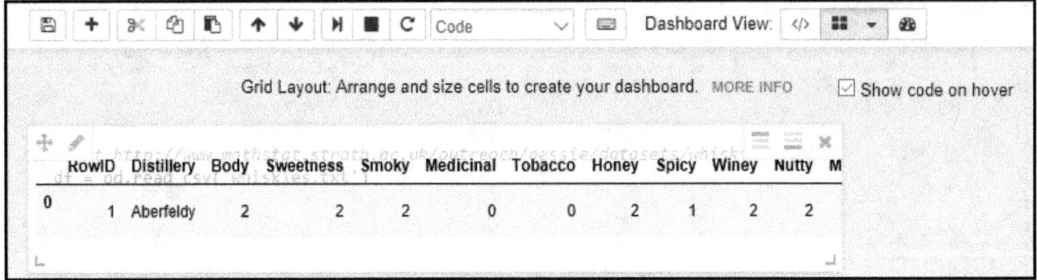

There are several icons added to the display to help you control your layout:

- The top of the screen tells you which layout you are in and provides a checkbox to halftone display the underlying code halftone to help you decide
- In the upper left of each item is a cross-hair positioning tool followed by an editing tool
- In the upper right of each item is an icon to position the item at the top of the grid, at the bottom of the grid or and an X to remove the item from the grid
- In all four corners of each item are sizing icons

The items that do not have a visual characteristic or have been removed from the display, they appear in a hidden section at the bottom of the page as shown:

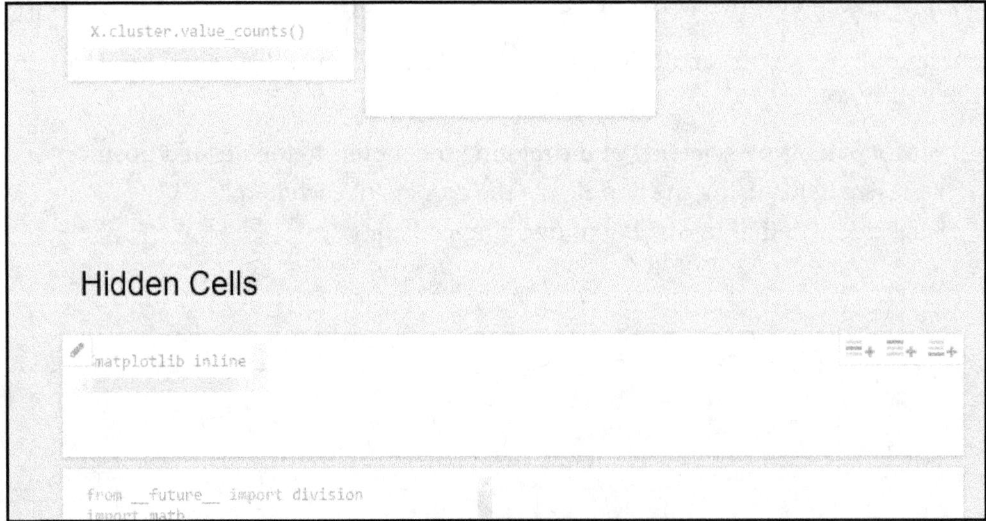

In **Dashboard Preview** mode, you see the dashboard as your readers will. The reader can move back to editing the Notebook, but the gadget menu is not visible, and the reader would have to be familiar with the menu system to understand how to do so. The menu during **Dashboard Preview** looks like the following:

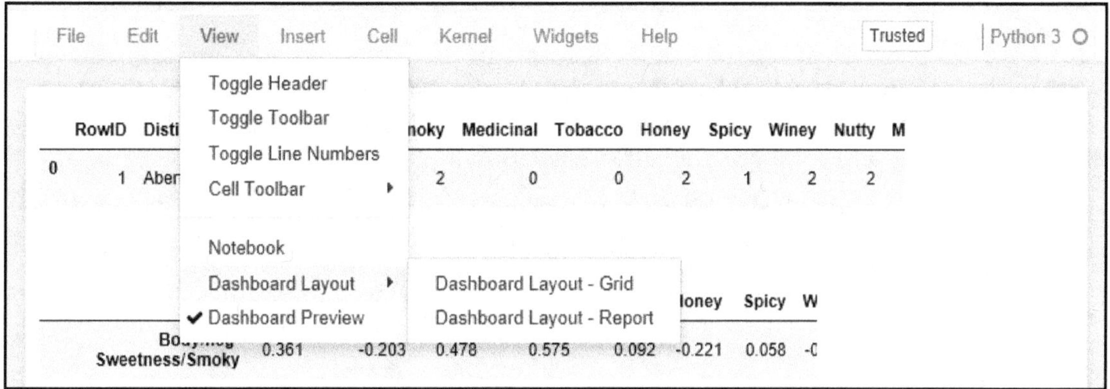

It allows the reader to move back to the normal Notebook view or to change layout.

It is important to note that the coding of the Notebook, in whatever language kernel is used, takes no adjustment to be displayed in a dashboard; all of that manipulation is handled by Jupyter without programmatic intervention.

There's more...

In the following sections, I am using a similar set of display sets from a fictitious business that sells grapefruits, using the different languages available. In all cases, a dashboard that provides information about sales for the company is presented. The data is provided at `http://www.dataapple.net/wp-content/uploads/2013/04/grapeJuice.csv`. In all forms, we present some latest details on sales, a regression analysis of the data, and some of the comparisons of ad usage.

Creating an R dashboard

In this section, we create a dashboard in an R Notebook.

How to do it...

We have the following script; it loads and analyzes the data, producing four graphical elements. They are the head of the dataset, regression analysis, comparing sales components as drivers to sales, and comparing ad effectiveness:

```
 # Load and display same of the data points
 #install.packages("s20x", repos='http://cran.us.r-project.org')
 #install.packages("car", repos='http://cran.us.r-project.org')

 # libraries used
 library(s20x)
 library(car)

 # load and display data - originally at
http://www.dataapple.net/wp-content/uploads/2013/04/
 df <- read.csv("grapeJuice.csv",header=T)
 head(df)
```

sales	price	ad_type	price_apple	price_cookies
222	9.83	0	7.36	8.80
201	9.72	1	7.43	9.62
247	10.15	1	7.66	8.90
169	10.04	0	7.57	10.26
317	8.38	1	7.33	9.54
227	9.74	0	7.51	9.49

```
# Calculate ad effectiveness
#
#divide the dataset into two sub dataset by ad_type
 sales_ad_nature = subset(df,ad_type==0)
 sales_ad_family = subset(df,ad_type==1)

# graph the two
 par(mfrow = c(1,2))
```

```
 hist(sales_ad_nature$sales,main="",xlab="sales with nature production
theme ad",prob=T)
 lines(density(sales_ad_nature$sales),lty="dashed",lwd=2.5,col="red")

 hist(sales_ad_family$sales,main="",xlab="sales with family health caring
theme ad",prob=T)
 lines(density(sales_ad_family$sales),lty="dashed",lwd=2.5,col="red")
```

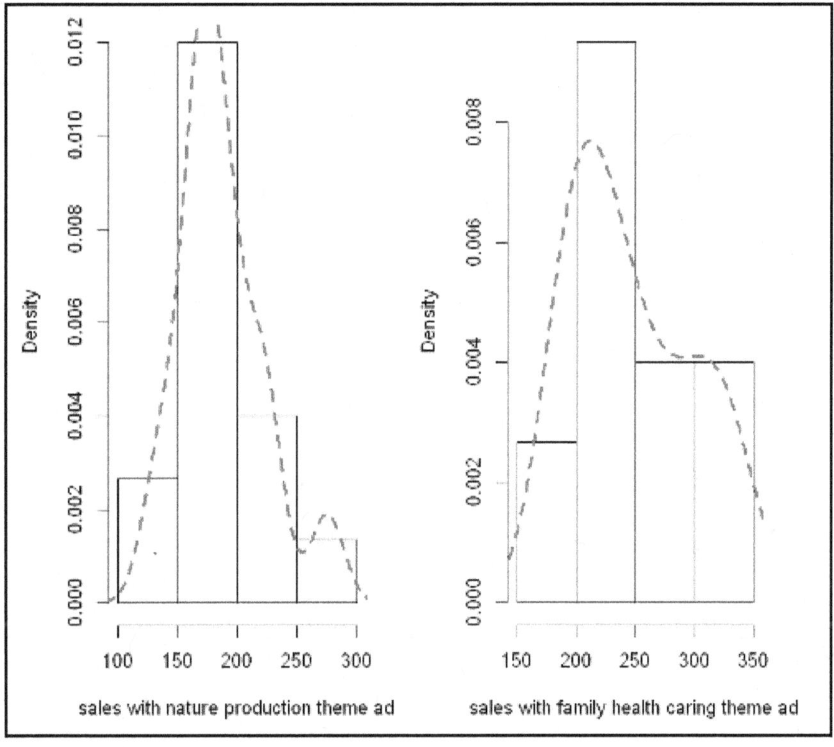

```
# Display Sales drivers
pairs20x(df)
```

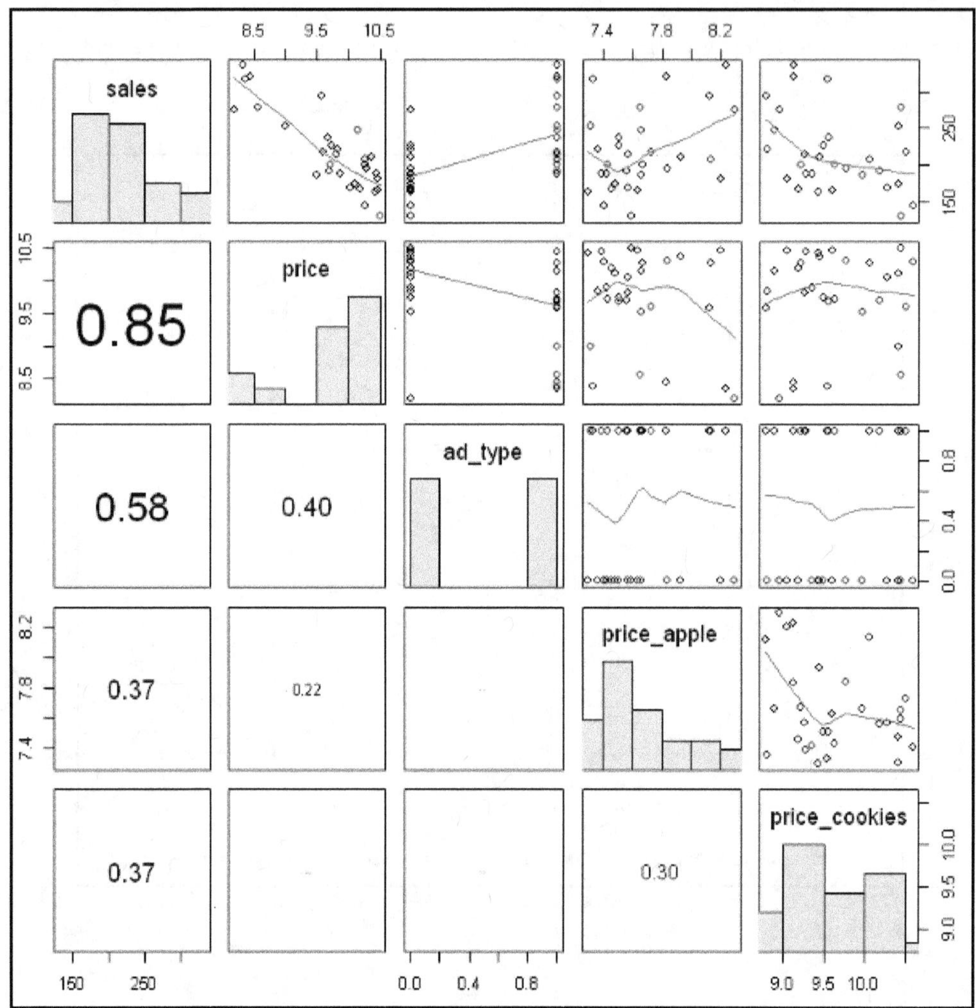

```
############################
# Regeression model on sales
#regression model
 sales.reg<-lm(sales~price+ad_type+price_apple+price_cookies,df)
 summary(sales.reg)
```

```
Call:
lm(formula = sales ~ price + ad_type + price_apple + price_cookies,
    data = df)

Residuals:
    Min      1Q  Median      3Q     Max
-36.290 -10.488   0.884  10.483  29.471

Coefficients:
              Estimate Std. Error t value Pr(>|t|)
(Intercept)    774.813    145.349   5.331 1.59e-05 ***
price          -51.239      5.321  -9.630 6.83e-10 ***
ad_type         29.742      7.249   4.103 0.000380 ***
price_apple     22.089     12.512   1.765 0.089710 .
price_cookies  -25.277      6.296  -4.015 0.000477 ***
---
Signif. codes:  0 '***' 0.001 '**' 0.01 '*' 0.05 '.' 0.1 ' ' 1

Residual standard error: 18.2 on 25 degrees of freedom
Multiple R-squared:  0.8974,    Adjusted R-squared:  0.881
F-statistic: 54.67 on 4 and 25 DF,  p-value: 5.318e-12
```

Once the Notebook is produced, we can switch to grid mode to lay out our dashboard to arrive at a screen that looks like the following:

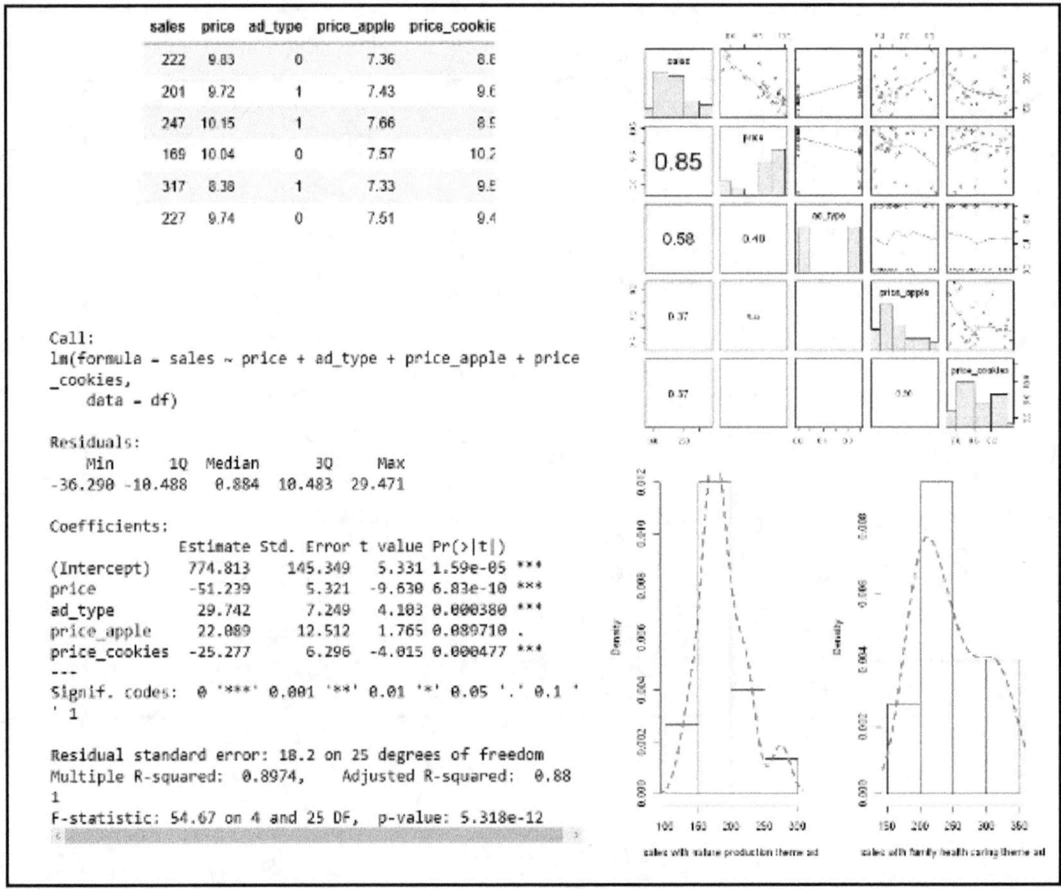

How it works...

The preceding graphics are pretty standard fare for R programming. The difference is that the dashboard enhancements to Jupyter allow you to arrange the R graphics as per your desired look.

Create a Python dashboard

We will use somewhat similar graphics and data derived from the same dataset as before to produce a dashboard based on Python coding.

How to do it...

We have the coding as follows.

We first load all the imports used. We also set up `matplotlib` to draw graphics inline in our Notebook. We also preconfigure the image sizes:

```
import pandas as pd
import numpy as np
import statsmodels.formula.api as sm
import matplotlib.pylab as plt
%matplotlib inline
from matplotlib.pylab import rcParams
rcParams['figure.figsize'] = 15, 6
```

We read in the data and display the first few records:

```
data = pd.read_csv("Documents/grapeJuice.csv")
data.head()
```

The following is the output:

	sales	price	ad_type	price_apple	price_cookies
0	222	9.83	0	7.36	8.80
1	201	9.72	1	7.43	9.62
2	247	10.15	1	7.66	8.90
3	169	10.04	0	7.57	10.26
4	317	8.38	1	7.33	9.54

We scale down the sales figures as the other factors are much smaller. Then we produce a scatter plot of the set:

```
data["sales"] = data["sales"] / 20
plt.plot(data); #suppresses extraneous matplotlib messages
```

The following is the output:

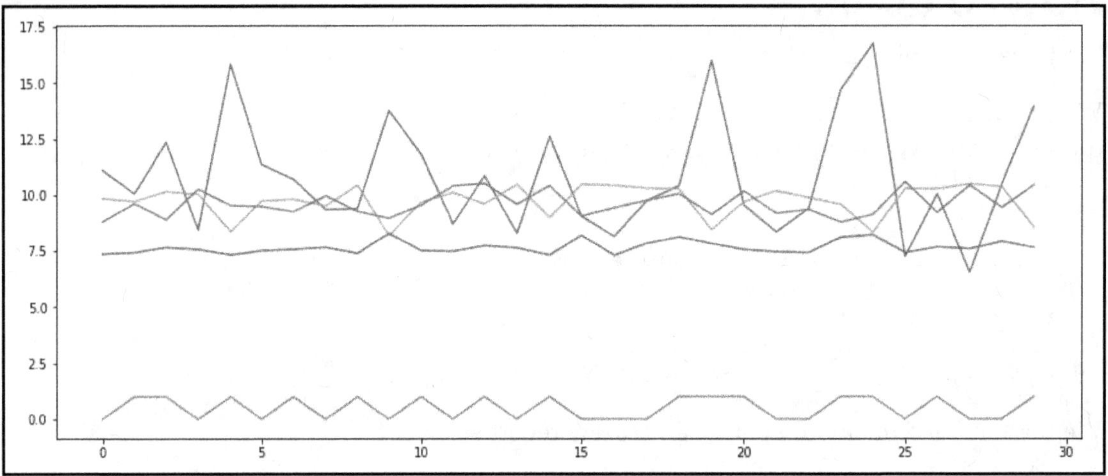

Next, we produce a regression analysis on the data:

```
Y = data['sales'][:-1]
X = data[['price','ad_type','price_apple','price_cookies']][:-1]
result = sm.OLS( Y, X ).fit()
result.summary()
```

OLS Regression Results

Dep. Variable:	sales	R-squared:	0.987
Model:	OLS	Adj. R-squared:	0.985
Method:	Least Squares	F-statistic:	493.2
Date:	Mon, 18 Dec 2017	Prob (F-statistic):	2.20e-23
Time:	22:31:35	Log-Likelihood:	-47.244
No. Observations:	29	AIC:	102.5
Df Residuals:	25	BIC:	108.0
Df Model:	4		
Covariance Type:	nonrobust		

	coef	std err	t	P>|t|	[0.025	0.975]
price	-1.8267	0.359	-5.089	0.000	-2.566	-1.087
ad_type	1.8703	0.520	3.599	0.001	0.800	2.941
price_apple	3.9575	0.475	8.339	0.000	2.980	4.935
price_cookies	-0.2758	0.391	-0.705	0.488	-1.082	0.530

Omnibus:	0.695	Durbin-Watson:	2.175
Prob(Omnibus):	0.706	Jarque-Bera (JB):	0.656
Skew:	0.327	Prob(JB):	0.720
Kurtosis:	2.661	Cond. No.	37.9

Then, after reorganizing the layout using the dashboard toolbar, we arrive at a layout like this:

	sales	price	ad_type	price_apple	price_cookies
0	222	9.83	0	7.36	8.80
1	201	9.72	1	7.43	9.62
2	247	10.15	1	7.66	8.90
3	169	10.04	0	7.57	10.26
4	317	8.38	1	7.33	9.54

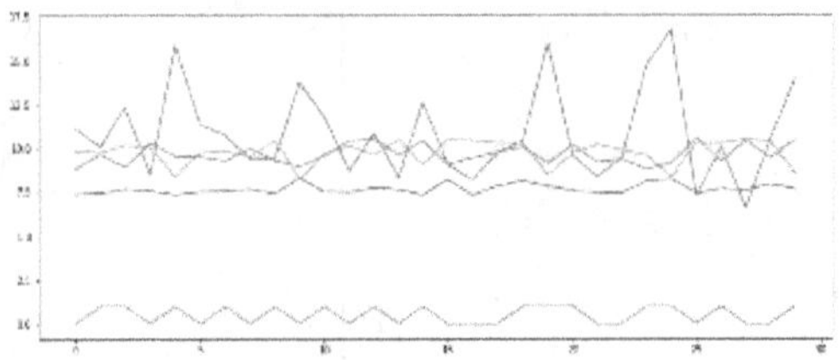

OLS Regression Results

Dep. Variable:	sales	**R-squared:**	0.987
Model:	OLS	**Adj. R-squared:**	0.985
Method:	Least Squares	**F-statistic:**	493.2
Date:	Mon, 18 Dec 2017	**Prob (F-statistic):**	2.20e-23
Time:	22:31:35	**Log-Likelihood:**	-47.244
No. Observations:	29	**AIC:**	102.5
Df Residuals:	25	**BIC:**	108.0
Df Model:	4		
Covariance Type:	nonrobust		

	coef	std err	t	P>|t|	[0.025	0.975]
price	-1.8267	0.359	-5.089	0.000	-2.566	-1.087
ad_type	1.8703	0.520	3.599	0.001	0.800	2.941
price_apple	3.9575	0.475	8.339	0.000	2.980	4.935
price_cookies	-0.2758	0.391	-0.705	0.488	-1.082	0.530

Omnibus:	0.695	**Durbin-Watson:**	2.175
Prob(Omnibus):	0.706	**Jarque-Bera (JB):**	0.656
Skew:	0.327	**Prob(JB):**	0.720
Kurtosis:	2.661	**Cond. No.**	37.9

Creating a Julia dashboard

In this section, we use a Julia Notebook to load a dataset, produce graphics, analyze the data, and put the entirety into a Jupyter Notebook.

How to do it...

Julia uses many of the packages available in R and/or Python, so the conversion is pretty similar.

Load in the packages used (again, very similar):

```
#Pkg.add("DataFrames")
#Pkg.add("PyPlot")
#Pkg.add("GLM")
using DataFrames;
using GLM;
using PyPlot;
```

Read in our `DataFrame` and look at the start of the table:

```
juice = readtable("grapeJuice.csv")
size(juice)
names(juice)
head(juice)
```

	sales	price	ad_type	price_apple	price_cookies
1	222	9.83	0	7.36	8.8
2	201	9.72	1	7.43	9.62
3	247	10.15	1	7.66	8.9
4	169	10.04	0	7.57	10.26
5	317	8.38	1	7.33	9.54
6	227	9.74	0	7.51	9.49

Produce a linear regression:

```
lm = fit(LinearModel, @formula(sales ~ price + ad_type + price_apple +
price_cookies), juice)
```

```
Formula: sales ~ 1 + price + ad_type + price_apple + price_cookies

Coefficients:
               Estimate Std.Error  t value Pr(>|t|)
(Intercept)     774.813   145.349   5.3307    <1e-4
price          -51.2393   5.32094 -9.62976    <1e-9
ad_type         29.7417   7.24851  4.10314   0.0004
price_apple     22.0892   12.5123   1.7654   0.0897
price_cookies  -25.2766   6.29589 -4.01478   0.0005
```

I found a Julia function to emulate the R `pairs()` functionality, which provides an x and y graph between all elements of a regression line from `https://gist.github.com/ahwillia/43c2cfb894f2bfec6760`:

```
function pairs(data)
    (nobs, nvars) = size(data)
    (fig, ax) = subplots(nvars, nvars, figsize=(8,8))
    subplots_adjust(hspace=0.05, wspace=0.05)

    # Plot data
    for i = 1:nvars
        for j = 1:nvars
            if i != j
                ax[i,j][:plot](data[:,j],data[:,i],"ob",mfc="none")
            else
                ax[i,j][:hist](data[:,i])
            end
            ax[i,j][:xaxis][:set_visible](false)
            ax[i,j][:yaxis][:set_visible](false)
        end
    end

    # Set tick positions
    for i = 1:nvars
        ax[i,1][:yaxis][:set_ticks_position]("left")
        ax[i,end][:yaxis][:set_ticks_position]("right")
        ax[1,i][:xaxis][:set_ticks_position]("top")
        ax[end,i][:xaxis][:set_ticks_position]("bottom")
    end

    # Turn ticks on
    cc = repmat([nvars, 1],Integer(ceil(nvars/2)),1)
    for i = 1:nvars
        ax[i,cc[i]][:yaxis][:set_visible](true)
        ax[cc[i],i][:xaxis][:set_visible](true)
    end
end
pairs(juice)
```

This produces our set of *x* and *y* scatter plots:

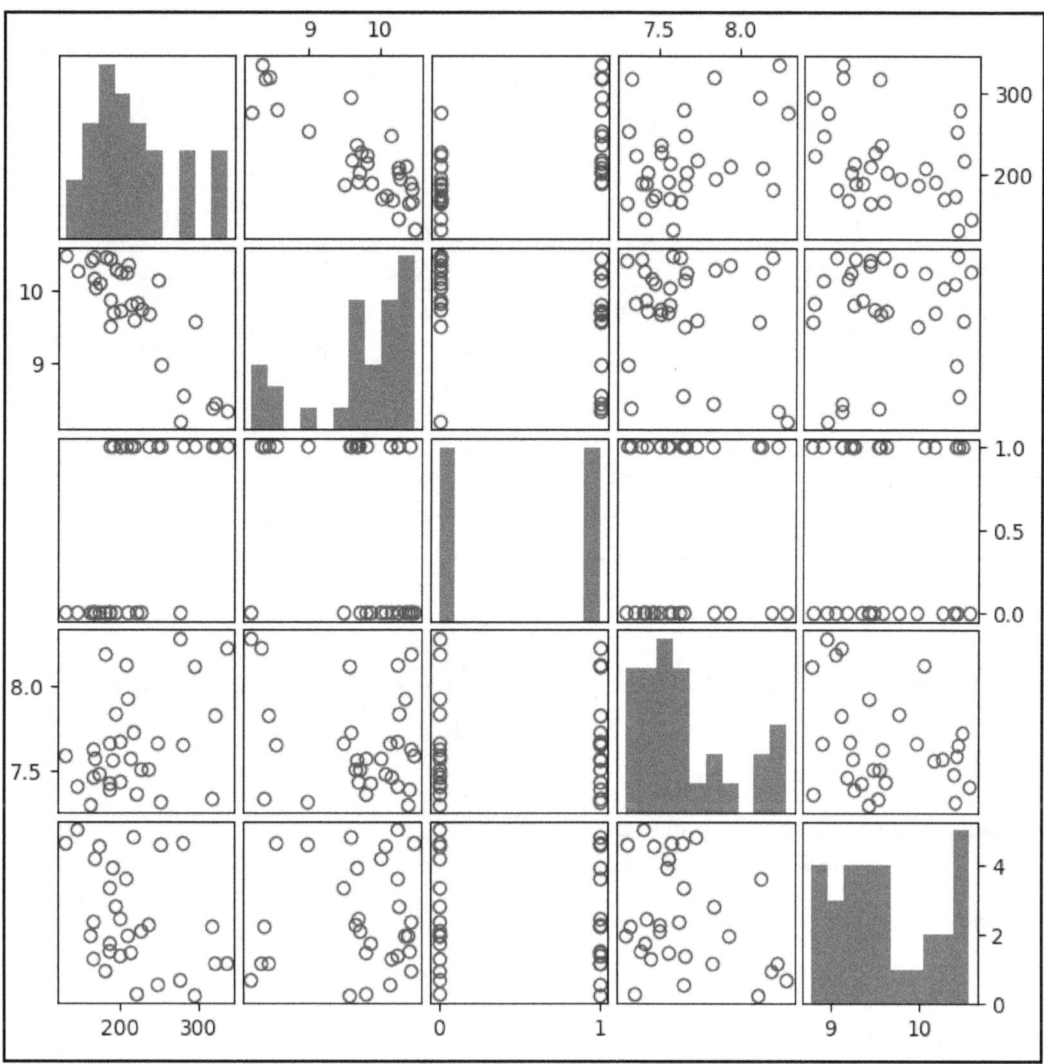

Then, rearranging under the dashboard, we see the display:

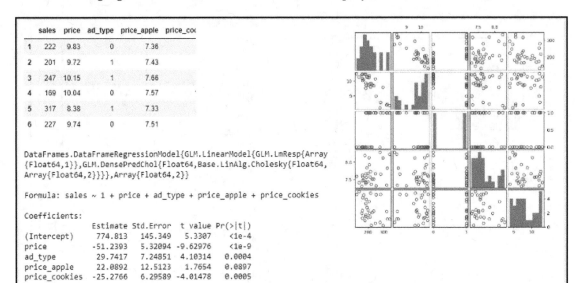

	sales	price	ad_type	price_apple	price_co(
1	222	9.83	0	7.36	
2	201	9.72	1	7.43	
3	247	10.15	1	7.66	
4	169	10.04	0	7.57	
5	317	8.38	1	7.33	
6	227	9.74	0	7.51	

```
DataFrames.DataFrameRegressionModel{GLM.LinearModel{GLM.LmResp{Array
{Float64,1}},GLM.DensePredChol{Float64,Base.LinAlg.Cholesky{Float64,
Array{Float64,2}}}},Array{Float64,2}}

Formula: sales ~ 1 + price + ad_type + price_apple + price_cookies

Coefficients:
               Estimate Std.Error  t value Pr(>|t|)
(Intercept)     774.813   145.349   5.3307    <1e-4
price          -51.2393   5.32094 -9.62976    <1e-9
ad_type         29.7417   7.24851  4.10314   0.0004
price_apple     22.0892   12.5123   1.7654   0.0897
price_cookies  -25.2766   6.29589 -4.01478   0.0005
```

Develop a JavaScript (Node.js) dashboard

In this section, we develop a `node.js` Notebook and change the presentation to a dashboard.

I could not get the JavaScript kernel to work on Windows. I used a Mac for this section.

How to do it...

We have two JavaScript sections in our Notebook that produce some statistics. In this first section, we read a TSV file, produce the corresponding JSON-formatted output on screen, and select the largest weight from the animal set in the file:

```
var fs = require("fs");
var d3 = require("d3");
var _ = require("lodash");
fs.readFile("/Users/ToomeyD/Documents//animals.tsv", "utf8",
```

```
function(error, data) {
     data = d3.tsvParse(data);
     console.log(JSON.stringify(data, null, 4));

     var maxWeight = d3.max(data, function(d) {
         return parseInt(d.avg_weight);
     });
     console.log(maxWeight);
});
```

This produces the output:

```
[
    {
        "name": "lion",
        "avg_weight": "400"
    },
    {
        "name": "tiger",
        "avg_weight": "400"
    },
    {
        "name": "human",
        "avg_weight": "150"
    },
    {
        "name": "elephant",
        "avg_weight": "2000"
    }
]
2000
```

And it produces a section computing basic statistics using the `stats` package:

```
const stats = require("stats-analysis");
var arr = [98, 98.6, 98.4, 98.8, 200, 120, 98.5];

//standard deviation
var my_stddev = stats.stdev(arr).toFixed(2);
//mean
var my_mean = stats.mean(arr).toFixed(2);
//median
var my_median = stats.median(arr);
//median absolute deviation
```

```
var my_mad = stats.MAD(arr);
// Get the index locations of the outliers in the data set
var my_outliers = stats.indexOfOutliers(arr);
// Remove the outliers
var my_without_outliers = stats.filterOutliers(arr);

//display our stats
console.log("Raw data is ", arr);
console.log("Standard Deviation is ", my_stddev);
console.log("Mean is ", my_mean);
console.log("Median is ", my_median);
console.log("Median Abs Deviation is " + my_mad);
console.log("The outliers of the data set are ", my_outliers);
console.log("The data set without outliers is ", my_without_outliers);
```

This is the output:

```
Raw data is  [ 98, 98.6, 98.4, 98.8, 200, 120, 98.5 ]
Standard Deviation is  35.07
Mean is  116.04
Median is  98.6
Median Abs Deviation is 0.20000000000000284
The outliers of the data set are  [ 4, 5, 6 ]
The data set without outliers is  [ 98, 98.6, 98.4, 98.8 ]
```

Both of these outputs are non-graphical, but they do take up space. We can rearrange them in a dashboard that looks like this:

```
[
    {
        "name": "lion",
        "avg_weight": "400"
    },
    {
        "name": "tiger",
        "avg_weight": "400"
    },
    {
        "name": "human",
        "avg_weight": "150"
    },
    {
        "name": "elephant",
        "avg_weight": "2000"
    }
]
2000
```

```
Raw data is  [ 98, 98.6, 98.4, 98.8, 200, 120, 98.5 ]
Standard Deviation is  35.07
Mean is  116.04
Median is  98.6
Median Abs Deviation is 0.20000000000000284
The outliers of the data set are  [ 4, 5, 6 ]
The data set without outliers is  [ 98, 98.6, 98.4, 98.8 ]
```

7
Sharing Your Code

In this chapter, we will cover the following recipes:

- Using a Notebook server
- Using a web server
- Sharing your Notebook through a public server
- Sharing your Notebook through Docker
- Sharing your Notebook using nbviewer
- Converting Notebooks to HTML
- Converting Notebooks to Markdown
- Converting Notebooks to reStructedText
- Converting Notebooks to Latex
- Converting Notebooks to PDF

Introduction

This chapter shows you several methods for sharing your Notebook with others, including using different software packages and converting the Notebook into a different form for readers without access to Jupyter.

Sharing your Notebook using server software

There are several software mechanisms available for sharing your Notebook with others. This section describes several of the currently available tools. I would expect the list to grow over time.

The typical mechanism for sharing Notebooks is to provide your Notebook on a website. A website runs on a server or allocated machine space. The server takes care of all the bookkeeping involved in running a website, such as keeping track of multiple users and logging people on and off.

In order for the Notebook to be of use, though, the website must have Notebook/Jupyter logic installed. A typical website knows how to deliver content as HTML given some source files. The most basic form is pure HTML, where every page you access on the website corresponds exactly to one HTML file on the web server. Other languages could be used to develop the website (such as Java or PHP); then the server needs to know how to access the HTML it needs from those source files. In our context, the server needs to know how to access our Notebook in order to deliver HTML to users.

Even when notebooks are just running on your local machine, they are running in a browser that is accessing your local machine (server) instead of the internet; so the web, HTML, and internet access has already been established.

If a Notebook is on true website, it is available to everyone who can access that website, whether the server is running on your machine in an office environment accessible over the local area network or your website is available to all users over the internet. You can always add security around the website so that the only people who can use your Notebook are those given access by you. Security mechanisms depend on the type of web server software involved.

Using a Notebook server

Built into the Jupyter process is the ability to expose a Notebook as its own web server. Assuming the server is a machine accessible by other users, you can configure Jupyter to run on that server. You must provide the configuration information to Jupyter so that it knows how to proceed. The command to generate a configuration file for your Jupyter installation is:

```
jupyter notebook --generate-config
```

This command will generate a `jupyter_notebook_config.py` file in your `~./jupyter` directory. For Microsoft users, that directory is a sub-directory of your home `User` directory.

The configuration file, shown as follows, contains the settings that you can use to expose your Notebook as a server:

```
c.NotebookApp.certfile = u'/path/to/your/cert/cert.pem'
c.NotebookApp.keyfile = u'/ path/to/your/cert/key.key'
c.NotebookApp.ip = '*'
c.NotebookApp.password = u'hashed-password'
c.NotebookApp.open_browser = False
c.NotebookApp.port = 8888
```

The following table describes each of the settings in the `config` file:

Setting	**Description/Usage**
`c.NotebookApp.certfile`	This is the path to the location of the certificate for your site. More information on certificate use follows. If you have an SSL certificate you need to change the setting to the location of the file. It may not be a `.PEM` extension file. There are several SSL certificate formats.
`c.NotebookApp.keyfile`	This is the path to the location of the key to access the cert for your site. Rather than specifying the key to your certificate, you will have stored the key in a file. So, if you want to apply an SSL certificate to your Notebook, you have to specify the file location. The key is normally a very large hexadecimal number. Hence it is stored in its own file. Also, storing it in a file offers additional protection as the directory where keys are stored on a machine is usually under limited access.
`c.NotebookApp.ip`	The IP address of the machine. Use the wildcard `*` to make it open to all. Here, we are specifying the IP address of the machine where the notebook website is accessed.
`c.NotebookApp.password`	Hashed password. The password will have to be provided by users accessing your notebook in response to a standard login challenge.
`c.NotebookApp.open_browser`	`True`/`False`. Does starting the notebook server open a browser window?
`c.NotebookApp.port`	Port to access your server. This should be open to the machine.

How to do it...

Once you have changed the settings appropriately, you should be able to point a browser at the URL configured and access your Notebook. The URL would be the concatenation of either HTTP or HTTPS (depending on whether you applied an SSL certificate), the IP address, and the port, for example, `HTTPS://123.45.56.9:8888`.

Using web encryption for your Notebook

Two of the aforementioned settings can be used if you have an SSL certificate to apply. Without the SSL certificate, the password (see the previous section) and all other interactions will be transmitted from the user's browser to the server in readable form. If you are dealing with sensitive information in your Notebook, you should obtain an SSL certificate and make the appropriate settings changes in your server.

If you need more security over access to your Notebook, the next step would be to provide an SSL certificate (placed on your machine and the path provided in the configuration file). There are a number of companies that provide SSL certificates. The cheapest as of this writing is let's encrypt, which will provide a low-level SSL certificate for free (there are gradations of SSL certificates that are not free).

Again, once you have made these settings in regard to your certificate, you should be able to access your Notebook server using the `HTTPS://` prefix, knowing that all transmissions between the user's browser and the Notebook server are encrypted and therefore secure.

Using a web server

So, built into Jupyter, you can access the configuration you need to expose a Jupyter Notebook on its own. If you were to take it to the next step and apply the Notebook to a regular web server, there would be just a few more steps in addition to the previous section.

How to do it...

In order to add your Notebook to an existing web server, you need to perform the preceding steps and add a little more information to the Notebook configuration file, as in:

```
c.NotebookApp.tornado_settings = {
 'headers': {
 'Content-Security-Policy': "frame-ancestors 'https://yourwebsite.com'
'self' "
 }
}
```

Replace `yourwebsite.com` with the URL of your website. Once complete, you can access the Notebook through your website.

Sharing your Notebook through a public server

Currently there is one hosting company that allows you to host your Notebooks for free: GitHub. GitHub is the standard web provider for source control (GIT source control) systems. Source control is used to maintain historical versions of your files to allow you to retrace your steps.

GitHub's implementation includes all the tools that you need to use in your Notebook, already installed on the server. For example, to use R programming in your Notebook, you would have had to install the R tool set on your machine and possibly some of the packages used by your script. But GitHub has already done all of these steps.

How to do it...

1. In order to host your Notebook on GitHub, go to the GitHub website and sign up for a free website.
2. Once logged in you are provided with a website that can be added to. If you have development tools to use (`git push` commands are programmer commands to store files on a git server) you can do that or simply drag and drop your Notebook (`ipynb`) file onto your GitHub website.

3. I created an account there, with a `notebooks` directory, and placed one of the `notebooks` on that site. My GitHub site looks like:

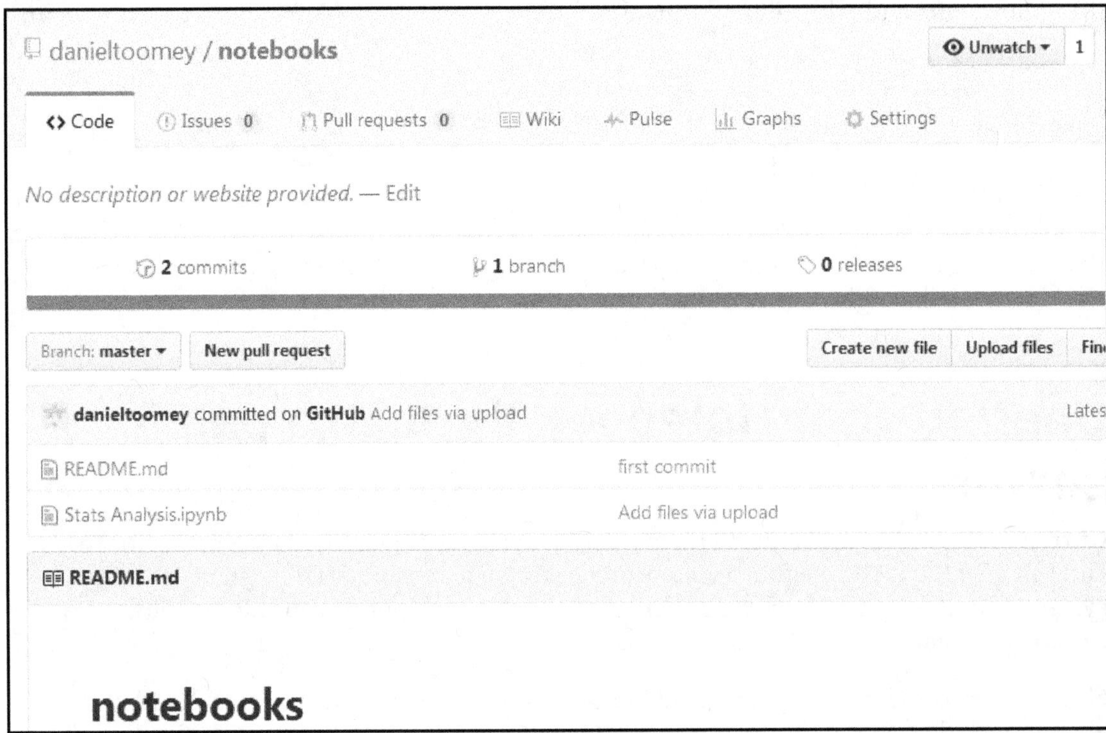

4. I have added a small Notebook script there, and as you can see in the following display, the Notebook executes as expected:

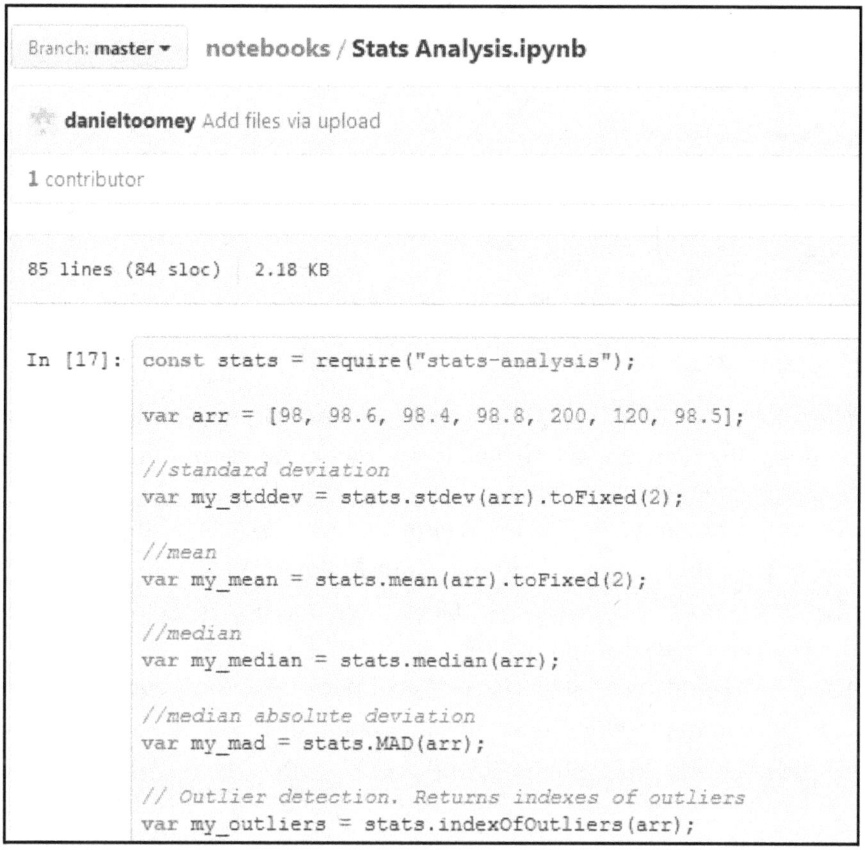

```
Branch: master ▾   notebooks / Stats Analysis.ipynb

danieltoomey Add files via upload

1 contributor

85 lines (84 sloc)   2.18 KB

In [17]: const stats = require("stats-analysis");

         var arr = [98, 98.6, 98.4, 98.8, 200, 120, 98.5];

         //standard deviation
         var my_stddev = stats.stdev(arr).toFixed(2);

         //mean
         var my_mean = stats.mean(arr).toFixed(2);

         //median
         var my_median = stats.median(arr);

         //median absolute deviation
         var my_mad = stats.MAD(arr);

         // Outlier detection. Returns indexes of outliers
         var my_outliers = stats.indexOfOutliers(arr);
```

Sharing your Notebook through Docker

Docker is an open lightweight container for distributing software. A typical Docker instance has an entire web server and a specific web application running on a machine (accessible through a specific port on the machine where Docker is running). In this manner, Docker can have many applications running on the machine, each addressable through a different port address.

How to do it...

The specifics about the software running in a Docker instance are governed by the Dockerfile. This file provides commands to the Docker environment as to which components to use to configure this instance. Sample Dockerfile contents for a Jupyter implementation would be:

```
ENV TINI_VERSION v0.6.0
ADD https://github.com/krallin/tini/releases/download/${TINI_VERSION}/tini
/usr/bin/tini
RUN chmod +x /usr/bin/tini
ENTRYPOINT ["/usr/bin/tini", "--"]
EXPOSE 8888
CMD ["jupyter", "notebook", "--port=8888", "--no-browser", "--ip=0.0.0.0"]
```

Here is a discussion on each of the commands of the Dockerfile:

- The `ENV` command tells Docker to use a specialized operating system. This is necessary to overcome a deficiency of Jupyter that keeps obtaining and releasing resources from your machine.
- The `ADD` command tells Docker where the `tini` code is located.
- The `RUN` command changes access rights to the `tini` directory.
- The `ENTRYPOINT` command tells Docker what to use as the operating system of the Docker instance, and now.
- The `EXPOSE` command tells Docker what port to expose your Notebook on.
- The `CMD` command tells Docker what commands to run (once the environment is set up). The `CMD` arguments are telling as you see the familiar `jupyter notebook` command that you use to start Jupyter on your machine.

Once the Docker instance is deployed to your Docker machine, you can access the Docker instance on the machine at the port specified (`8888`), for example, `http://machinename.com:8888`.

The preceding instructions assume you are new to Docker. If you already have an existing Docker installation, the instructions may be different for your environment.

Sharing your Notebook using nbviewer

Built into Jupyter is a tool called `nbviewer`, responsible for exposing your Notebook as a web page. `nbviewer` is used through a public Notebook sharing service, the Notebook Viewer, at `http://nbviewer.ipython.org`.

`nbviewer` is fully supported by the Jupyter project. So, if you encounter any issues they will help.

You can use `nbviewer` in conjunction with Docker or standalone.

How to do it...

To use `nbviewer` with Docker, you can use Docker commands directly to load your Notebook:

```
$ docker pull jupyter/nbviewer
$ docker run -p 8080:8080 jupyter/nbviewer
```

These commands are as follows:

- The `docker pull` command downloads `nbviewer` from the code repository where all Jupyter products are maintained onto your machine
- The `docker run` command executes `nbviewer` (just downloaded) and exposes Jupyter at port `8080` (which is a standard HTTP port address)

Once executed, if you open a browser to the local machine and port `8080`, you see the standard Jupyter home page. You can then add your Notebook as before.

You can run `nbviewer` on its own as well using the commands:

```
$ cd <path to notebook(s)>
$ python -m nbviewer --debug --no-cache
```

The command runs Python with the `nbviewer` module. The additional flags are optional:

- `--debug` to produce debug information on the command screen
- `--no-cache` to operate without cached results (so, pages are continually regenerated)

This will expose the `notebook(s)` in the directory that you changed to. The Notebook display will not change until you restart the `nbviewer` program.

This setup did not work on a Windows machine.

Converting your Notebook into a different format

Another mechanism is to convert your Notebook into a different, normally non-interactive format. This allows you to distribute the Notebook result to users without access to your server. A Notebook can be converted to a set of formats discussed in this section.

Sharing your Notebook using kyso: kyso is a Notebook sharing site particularly for scientists to exchange Notebook information.
I do not think it would be a good idea for me to push a sample Notebook onto the site.
You can get various sorts of subscription access to kyso.

How to do it...

For the conversions, we will be using a minimal R script that describes the `iris` dataset. The code is:

```
data(iris)
head(iris)
summary(iris)
plot(iris)
```

Producing the now-familiar data points for the `iris` set and the corresponding plot:

```
data(iris)
head iris
```

Sepal.Length	Sepal.Width	Petal.Length	Petal.Width	Species
5.1	3.5	1.4	0.2	setosa
4.9	3.0	1.4	0.2	setosa
4.7	3.2	1.3	0.2	setosa
4.6	3.1	1.5	0.2	setosa
5.0	3.6	1.4	0.2	setosa
5.4	3.9	1.7	0.4	setosa

```
summary(iris)
```

```
  Sepal.Length    Sepal.Width     Petal.Length    Petal.Width   
 Min.   :4.300   Min.   :2.000   Min.   :1.000   Min.   :0.100  
 1st Qu.:5.100   1st Qu.:2.800   1st Qu.:1.600   1st Qu.:0.300  
 Median :5.800   Median :3.000   Median :4.350   Median :1.300  
 Mean   :5.843   Mean   :3.057   Mean   :3.758   Mean   :1.199  
 3rd Qu.:6.400   3rd Qu.:3.300   3rd Qu.:5.100   3rd Qu.:1.800  
 Max.   :7.900   Max.   :4.400   Max.   :6.900   Max.   :2.500  
       Species  
 setosa    :50  
 versicolor:50  
 virginica :50  
```

With the corresponding graph of the `iris` data:

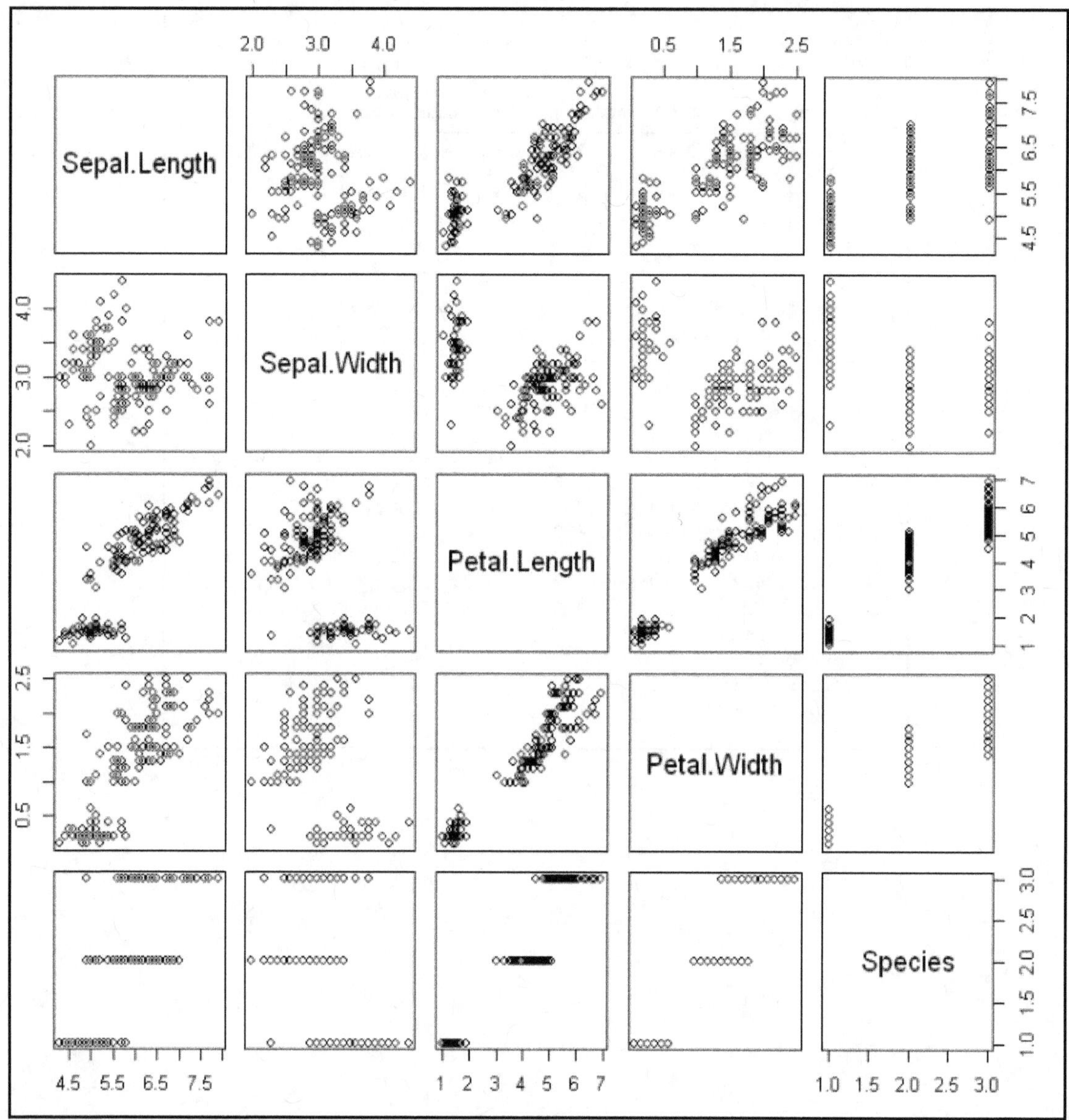

We will be using the Jupyter **File** menu options for this section, as you can see here:

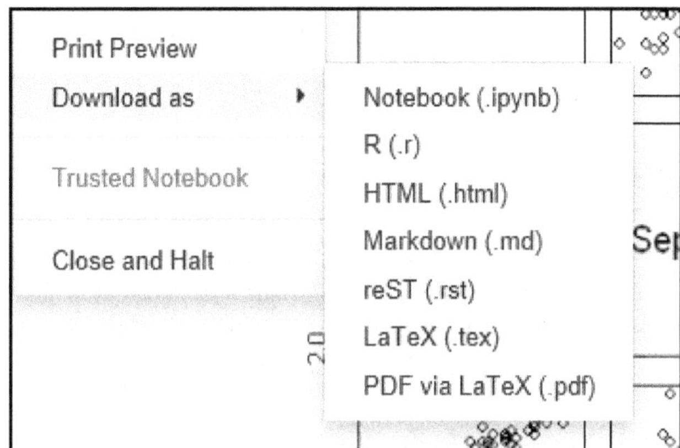

Where the choices listed are:

- **Notebook**: This is used to download the Notebook file (it has an `ipnyb` file extension). If you were running Jupyter off a server in the network, you could get a copy of the Notebook file in this manner. Once you have the Notebook file, you can use Jupyter elsewhere to run the main menu `File Upload` command (near the top right of the Jupyter screen) to upload your Notebook onto a different Jupyter instance.
- **R**: The section menu choice in the **Download As** menu corresponds to the language engine being used for the Notebook, in this case, R.
- **HTML**: Download an HTML representation of the Notebook.
- **Markdown**: Download a Markdown (similar to HTML) representation of the Notebook.
- **reST**: Obtain the restructed text format (an older format).
- **LaTeX**: Latex is a commonly used, older graphic format.
- **PDF**: We have all seen PDF files.

Converting Notebooks to R

Again, this section corresponds to the language choice in use for the Notebook. The choice downloads an R file from Jupyter to your machine.

How to do it...

You are on the Notebook in Jupyter. Selecting the choice will prompt for a location and then Jupyter will extract the Notebook code to the location specified using a filename containing the title of the Notebook with an R extension. In this case, the file was named `B09656_07+r+iris+for+conversions.r`, where I had titled the Notebook `B09656_07 r iris for conversions`.

How it works...

1. We can open the downloaded R script, and we have just the R script in the Notebook:

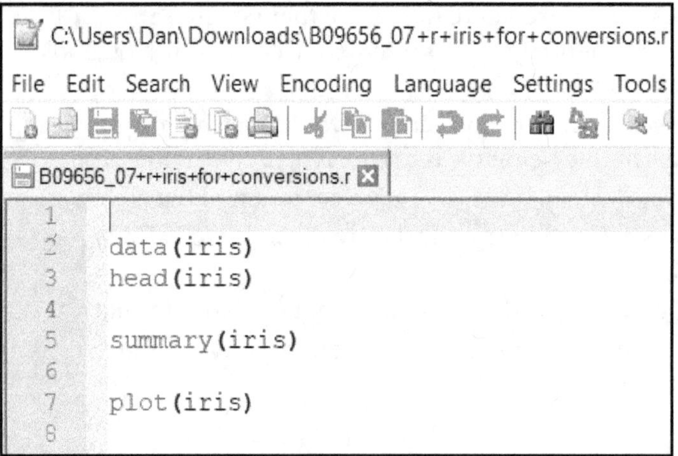

2. So, as it is a good R script, we can run it. I had already installed Anaconda with the corresponding R Studio. So, I ran the script in R studio with the expected result:

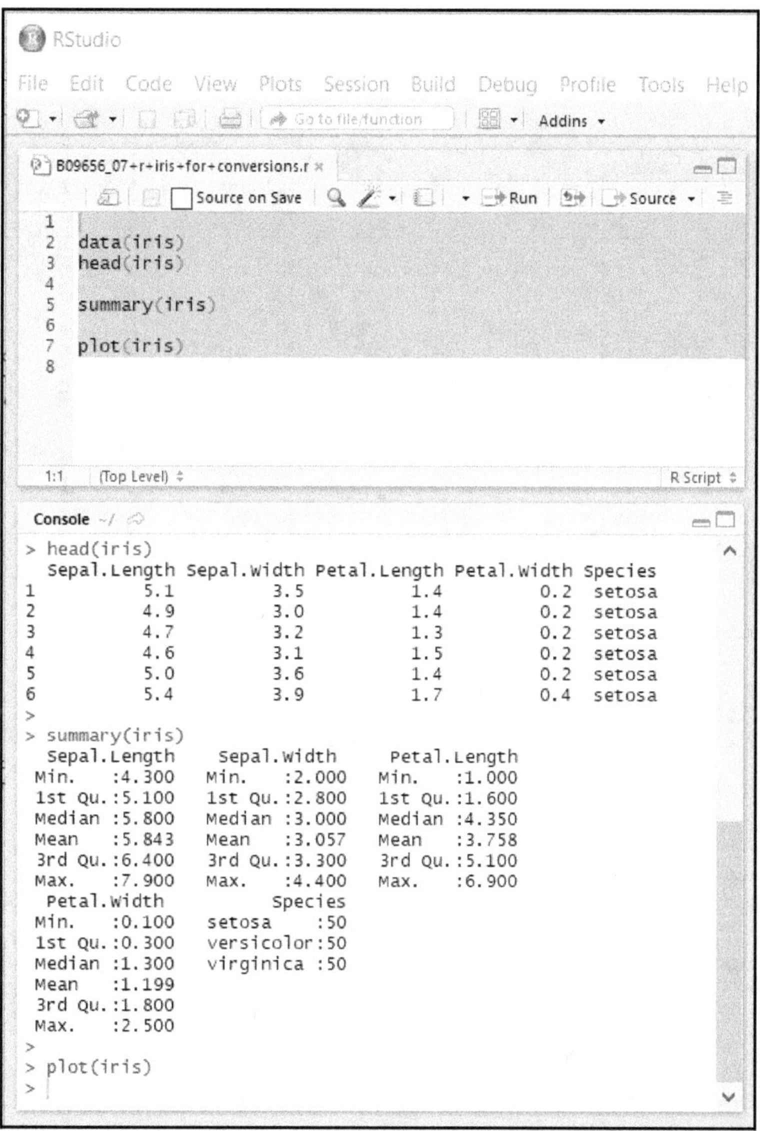

3. The graphic is in a pop-up window for R Studio:

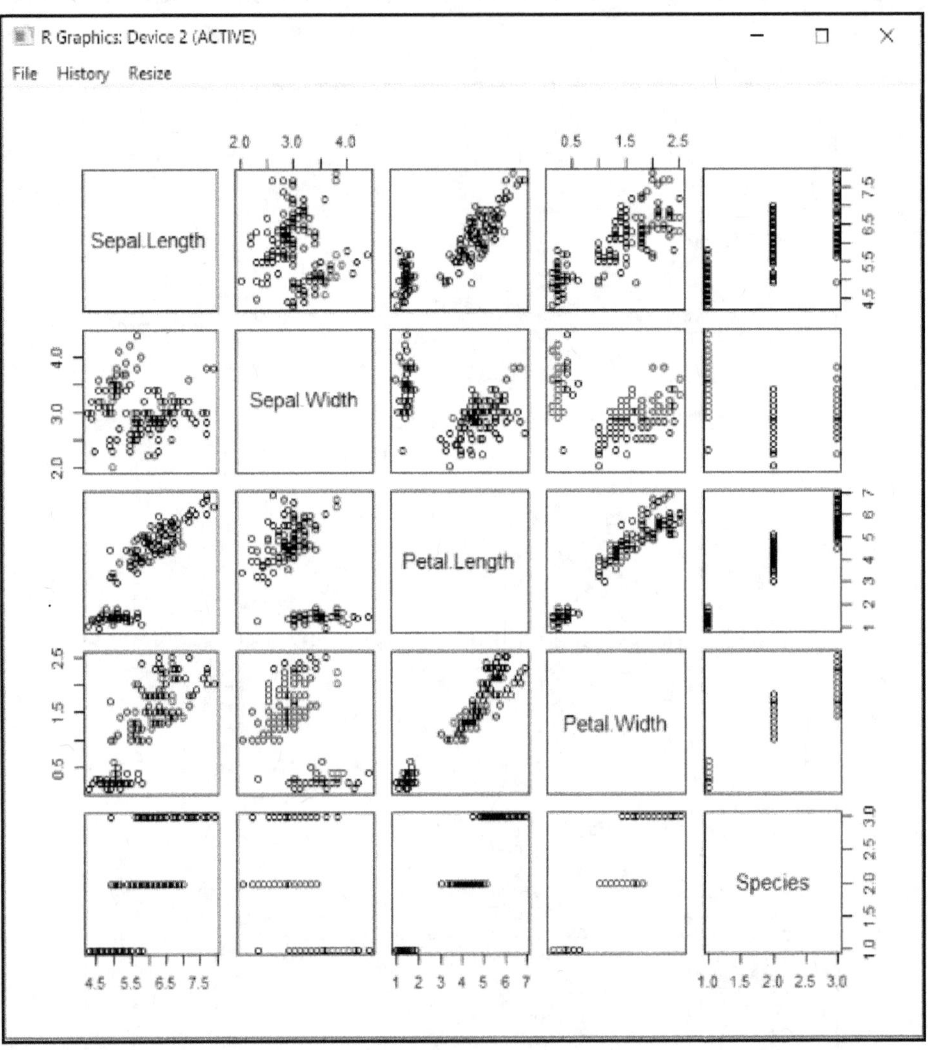

Converting Notebooks to HTML

We can also download an HTML version of the Notebook.

How to do it...

Similar to the other formats, once we have the Notebook open in Jupyter, we can extract an HTML representation by the appropriate selection from the menu. The system will prompt you for a location for the download.

How it works...

The Notebook will be downloaded to a filename with the Notebook title and the extension HTML. In my case, the file was called `B09656_07+r+iris+for+conversions.html`.

As with any HTML file, we can open and display it using a browser. In this case, I ended up with a display like the following:

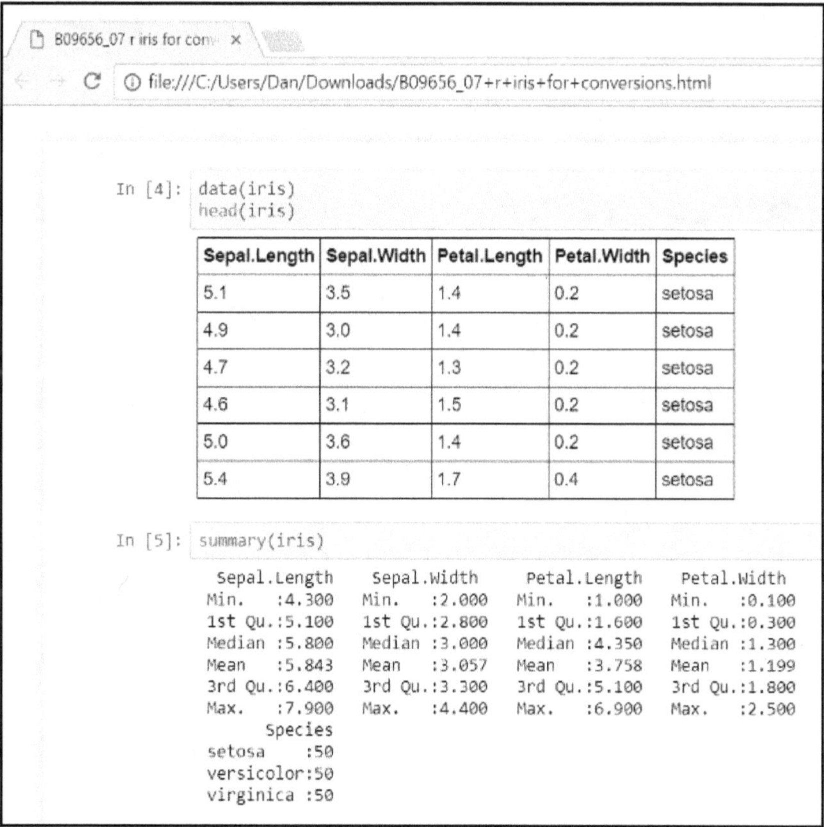

Sepal.Length	Sepal.Width	Petal.Length	Petal.Width	Species
5.1	3.5	1.4	0.2	setosa
4.9	3.0	1.4	0.2	setosa
4.7	3.2	1.3	0.2	setosa
4.6	3.1	1.5	0.2	setosa
5.0	3.6	1.4	0.2	setosa
5.4	3.9	1.7	0.4	setosa

With the following graphic further down the page:

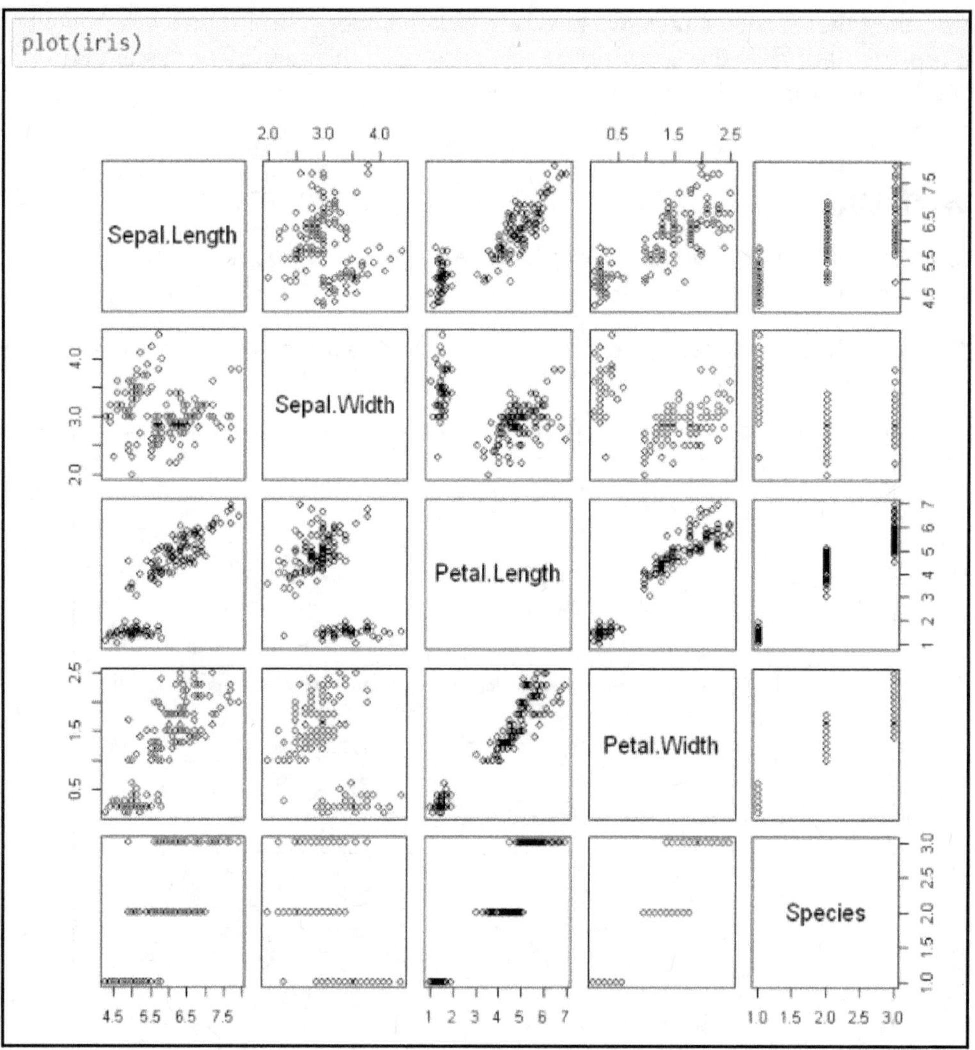

So, it looks exactly the same. There is no interactivity though.

I was curious about the contents of the downloaded HTML file and saw code like this:

```
<div class="output_text output_subarea ">
<pre>  Sepal.Length    Sepal.Width     Petal.Length    Petal.Width
 Min.   :4.300   Min.   :2.000   Min.   :1.000   Min.   :0.100
 1st Qu.:5.100   1st Qu.:2.800   1st Qu.:1.600   1st Qu.:0.300
 Median :5.800   Median :3.000   Median :4.350   Median :1.300
 Mean   :5.843   Mean   :3.057   Mean   :3.758   Mean   :1.199
 3rd Qu.:6.400   3rd Qu.:3.300   3rd Qu.:5.100   3rd Qu.:1.800
 Max.   :7.900   Max.   :4.400   Max.   :6.900   Max.   :2.500
       Species
 setosa    :50
 versicolor:50
 virginica :50


               </pre>


<div class="output_png output_subarea ">
<img src="data:image/png;base64,iVBORw0KGgoAAAANSUhEUgAAA0gAAANICAMAAADKOT
jIyampqnp6eysrK9vb3Hx8fQ0NDZ2dnh4eHp6enw8PD////QFLu4AAAACXBIWXMAABJ0AAAS
dAHeZh94AAAgAElEQVR4nO1diZajOAx0n9PbPdP8/99uEsCnLF8CBKl6uxkuS4XtsmVB0mYC
AGAY5mgCAHAFQEgAIAAICQAEACEBgAAgJAAQAIQEAAKAkABAABASAAgAQgIAAUBIACAACAkA
BAAhAYAAICQAEACEBAACgJAAQAAQEgAIAEICAAFASAAgAAgJAAQAIQGAACAkABAAhAQAAoCQ
```

The results are laid out as they were shown in Jupyter. The follow-on `img` tag at the bottom of the screenshot is the `hex` storage format of the generated graphic.

Converting Notebooks to Markdown

The Markdown (files with `.md` extension) format is a looser version of HTML, which is another Markdown format. The `README` files of many software distribution packages are stored in Markdown format.

How to do it...

Once we have a Notebook in use in Jupyter, we can select the **Download Markdown** menu choice. As with others, Jupyter prompts you for the location to store the file.

How it works...

The downloaded Markdown file is named with the name of your Notebook followed by the file extension `.zip`, as there are multiple components to the Markdown. Using the same example, my download was named `B09656_07+r+iris+for+conversions.zip`. In my `.zip` file, there were:

- `B09656_07 r iris for conversions.md`: The Markdown file
- `output_2_0.png`: The corresponding graphic

If we use an `md` file viewer (there are many available), we get a familiar-looking screenshot:

Sepal.Length	Sepal.Width	Petal.Length	Petal.Width	Species
5.1	3.5	1.4	0.2	setosa
4.9	3.0	1.4	0.2	setosa
4.7	3.2	1.3	0.2	setosa
4.6	3.1	1.5	0.2	setosa
5.0	3.6	1.4	0.2	setosa
5.4	3.9	1.7	0.4	setosa

```
summary(iris)
```

```
 Sepal.Length    Sepal.Width     Petal.Length    Petal.Width
Min.   :4.300   Min.   :2.000   Min.   :1.000   Min.   :0.100
1st Qu.:5.100   1st Qu.:2.800   1st Qu.:1.600   1st Qu.:0.300
```

And the corresponding graphic is an exact match.

Looking inside of the `.md` file, we see a lot of HTML tags used for the table layout of the `head` command and then some Markdown-formatted information (for the `summary` output):

````
```R
data(iris)
head(iris)
```
<table>
<thead><tr><th scope=col>Sepal.Length</th><th scope=col>Sepal.Width</th><th scope=col>Pet
<tbody>
    <tr><td>5.1   </td><td>3.5   </td><td>1.4   </td><td>0.2   </td><td>setosa</td></tr>
    <tr><td>4.9   </td><td>3.0   </td><td>1.4   </td><td>0.2   </td><td>setosa</td></tr>
    <tr><td>4.7   </td><td>3.2   </td><td>1.3   </td><td>0.2   </td><td>setosa</td></tr>
    <tr><td>4.6   </td><td>3.1   </td><td>1.5   </td><td>0.2   </td><td>setosa</td></tr>
    <tr><td>5.0   </td><td>3.6   </td><td>1.4   </td><td>0.2   </td><td>setosa</td></tr>
    <tr><td>5.4   </td><td>3.9   </td><td>1.7   </td><td>0.4   </td><td>setosa</td></tr>
</tbody>
</table>

```R
summary(iris)
```
      Sepal.Length    Sepal.Width     Petal.Length    Petal.Width   
     Min.   :4.300   Min.   :2.000   Min.   :1.000   Min.   :0.100  
     1st Qu.:5.100   1st Qu.:2.800   1st Qu.:1.600   1st Qu.:0.300  
     Median :5.800   Median :3.000   Median :4.350   Median :1.300  
     Mean   :5.843   Mean   :3.057   Mean   :3.758   Mean   :1.199  
     3rd Qu.:6.400   3rd Qu.:3.300   3rd Qu.:5.100   3rd Qu.:1.800  
     Max.   :7.900   Max.   :4.400   Max.   :6.900   Max.   :2.500  
           Species  
     setosa    :50  
     versicolor:50  
     virginica :50  

```R
plot(iris)
```
![png](output_2_0.png)
````

Converting Notebooks to reStructedText

The reStructuredText (`.rst`) format is a simple, plain-text markup language that is used for programming documentation.

How to do it...

With the Notebook loaded into Jupyter, you can select the **Download** reST format file. You are then prompted to handle the download to your machine.

How it works...

As with some of the other downloads, the downloaded file is in `.zip` format, containing the `.rst` file and a `.png` of the graphic. The files are all named as the name of the Notebook followed by the appropriate extension (`.zip`, `.rst`, and `.png`). My files used the Notebook name of `B09656_07+r+iris+for+conversions`.

There are many `.rst` file viewers available. In the one I picked, the display looks like:

```
data(iris)
head(iris)
```

Sepal.Length	Sepal.Width	Petal.Length	Petal.Width	Species
5.1	3.5	1.4	0.2	setosa
4.9	3.0	1.4	0.2	setosa
4.7	3.2	1.3	0.2	setosa
4.6	3.1	1.5	0.2	setosa
5.0	3.6	1.4	0.2	setosa
5.4	3.9	1.7	0.4	setosa

```
summary(iris)
```

```
  Sepal.Length    Sepal.Width     Petal.Length    Petal.Width   
Min.   :4.300   Min.   :2.000   Min.   :1.000   Min.   :0.100  
1st Qu.:5.100   1st Qu.:2.800   1st Qu.:1.600   1st Qu.:0.300  
Median :5.800   Median :3.000   Median :4.350   Median :1.300  
Mean   :5.843   Mean   :3.057   Mean   :3.758   Mean   :1.199  
3rd Qu.:6.400   3rd Qu.:3.300   3rd Qu.:5.100   3rd Qu.:1.800  
Max.   :7.900   Max.   :4.400   Max.   :6.900   Max.   :2.500  
       Species  
setosa    :50  
versicolor:50  
```

Which, I think, is one of the better renderings of this information.

The plot graphic `.png` is also included; it looks as shown earlier.

The internals of the `.rst` file look like a combination of HTML and markup:

```
.. code:: r

    data(iris)
    head(iris)

.. raw:: html

    <table>
    <thead><tr><th scope=col>Sepal.Length</th><th scope=col>Sepal.Width</th><th
scope=col>Petal.Length</th><th scope=col>Petal.Width</th><th scope=col>Species</th>
</tr></thead>
    <tbody>
        <tr><td>5.1    </td><td>3.5    </td><td>1.4    </td><td>0.2
</td><td>setosa</td></tr>
        <tr><td>4.9    </td><td>3.0    </td><td>1.4    </td><td>0.2
</td><td>setosa</td></tr>
        <tr><td>4.7    </td><td>3.2    </td><td>1.3    </td><td>0.2
</td><td>setosa</td></tr>
        <tr><td>4.6    </td><td>3.1    </td><td>1.5    </td><td>0.2
</td><td>setosa</td></tr>
        <tr><td>5.0    </td><td>3.6    </td><td>1.4    </td><td>0.2
</td><td>setosa</td></tr>
        <tr><td>5.4    </td><td>3.9    </td><td>1.7    </td><td>0.4
</td><td>setosa</td></tr>
    </tbody>
    </table>
.. code:: r

    summary(iris)
```

This is similar to other generated formats, especially HTML. There are slightly different layout commands, for example, `. . code:: r`.

Converting Notebooks to Latex

Latex is a typesetting system that has been in use for some time. It is widely used for scholastic papers.

How to do it...

We can download a Latex version of the Notebook from the **File Download** menu. There will be a resulting `.zip` file downloaded to your machine. The filename will be the name of your Notebook, in this case, `B09656_07+r+iris+for+conversions`. The `.zip` file contains:

- `B09656_07+r+iris+for+conversions.tex`: The Latex file
- `output_2_0.png`: The corresponding graphic

How it works...

There are many Latex viewers (and editors) available. The display of my downloaded Latex file looks like:

B09656_07 r iris for conversions

January 1, 2018

```
In [4]: data(iris)
        head(iris)
```

Sepal.Length	Sepal.Width	Petal.Length	Petal.Width	Species
5.1	3.5	1.4	0.2	setosa
4.9	3.0	1.4	0.2	setosa
4.7	3.2	1.3	0.2	setosa
4.6	3.1	1.5	0.2	setosa
5.0	3.6	1.4	0.2	setosa
5.4	3.9	1.7	0.4	setosa

```
In [5]: summary(iris)

  Sepal.Length    Sepal.Width     Petal.Length    Petal.Width
 Min.   :4.300   Min.   :2.000   Min.   :1.000   Min.   :0.100
 1st Qu.:5.100   1st Qu.:2.800   1st Qu.:1.600   1st Qu.:0.300
 Median :5.800   Median :3.000   Median :4.350   Median :1.300
 Mean   :5.843   Mean   :3.057   Mean   :3.758   Mean   :1.199
 3rd Qu.:6.400   3rd Qu.:3.300   3rd Qu.:5.100   3rd Qu.:1.800
 Max.   :7.900   Max.   :4.400   Max.   :6.900   Max.   :2.500
       Species
 setosa    :50
 versicolor:50
 virginica :50
```

I think it looks very much like one of the papers you might see published by a college.

The plot graphic `.png` is also included; it looks as shown earlier.

The underlying code is very specific to Latex. I don't imagine anyone would normally work directly with Latex, but they would use a graphical editor that generates Latex to develop pages:

```

    \begin{Verbatim}[commandchars=\\\{\}]
{\color{incolor}In [{\color{incolor}4}]:} data\PY{p}{(}iris\PY{p}{)}
        \PY{k+kp}{head}\PY{p}{(}iris\PY{p}{)}
\end{Verbatim}


    \begin{tabular}{r|lllll}
 Sepal.Length & Sepal.Width & Petal.Length & Petal.Width & Species\\
\hline
     5.1    & 3.5    & 1.4    & 0.2    & setosa\\
     4.9    & 3.0    & 1.4    & 0.2    & setosa\\
     4.7    & 3.2    & 1.3    & 0.2    & setosa\\
     4.6    & 3.1    & 1.5    & 0.2    & setosa\\
     5.0    & 3.6    & 1.4    & 0.2    & setosa\\
     5.4    & 3.9    & 1.7    & 0.4    & setosa\\
\end{tabular}



    \begin{Verbatim}[commandchars=\\\{\}]
{\color{incolor}In [{\color{incolor}5}]:} \PY{k+kp}{summary}\PY{p}{(}iris\PY{p}{)}
\end{Verbatim}



    \begin{verbatim}
  Sepal.Length    Sepal.Width     Petal.Length    Petal.Width
 Min.   :4.300   Min.   :2.000   Min.   :1.000   Min.   :0.100
 1st Qu.:5.100   1st Qu.:2.800   1st Qu.:1.600   1st Qu.:0.300
 Median :5.800   Median :3.000   Median :4.350   Median :1.300
 Mean   :5.843   Mean   :3.057   Mean   :3.758   Mean   :1.199
 3rd Qu.:6.400   3rd Qu.:3.300   3rd Qu.:5.100   3rd Qu.:1.800
 Max.   :7.900   Max.   :4.400   Max.   :6.900   Max.   :2.500
       Species
 setosa    :50
 versicolor:50
 virginica :50



    \end{verbatim}


    \begin{Verbatim}[commandchars=\\\{\}]
{\color{incolor}In [{\color{incolor}6}]:} plot\PY{p}{(}iris\PY{p}{)}
\end{Verbatim}

```

Converting Notebooks to PDF

Lastly, we can download a PDF version of the Notebook. With the name of the menu item `''`, I would expect the resulting PDF to look very much like the Latex version in the previous section.

How to do it...

With our Notebook loaded into Jupyter, we can select to **Download PDF** menu choice. We will be prompted to handle the download file.

How it works...

Surprisingly, this did not work. I got a **500** error when I tried to download the PDF:

500 : Internal Server Error

The error was:

```
nbconvert failed: xelatex not found on PATH, if you have not installed xelatex you may need to do so. Find fu
rther instructions at https://nbconvert.readthedocs.io/en/latest/install.html#installing-tex.
```

It turns out that the name of the menu choice, `PDF via Latex`, is indicative of the failure. We need to install software that can take a Latex file and generate a PDF. Following along the URL mentioned in the failure message (`https://nbconvert.readthedocs.io/en/latest/install.html#installing-tex`), there are instructions for installing Latex on different operating systems. After installing, you need to stop and restart Jupyter for the new software to take effect.

Trying again after installing Latex, the resulting PDF file name uses the name of the Notebook with the PDF extension. In this case, the filename is `B09656_07+r+iris+for+conversions.pdf`. Once downloaded, I could view the PDF file (I used Acrobat viewer) with the resulting display:

B09656_07 r iris for conversions

January 1, 2018

```
In [4]: data(iris)
        head(iris)
```

Sepal.Length	Sepal.Width	Petal.Length	Petal.Width	Species
5.1	3.5	1.4	0.2	setosa
4.9	3.0	1.4	0.2	setosa
4.7	3.2	1.3	0.2	setosa
4.6	3.1	1.5	0.2	setosa
5.0	3.6	1.4	0.2	setosa
5.4	3.9	1.7	0.4	setosa

```
In [5]: summary(iris)

  Sepal.Length    Sepal.Width     Petal.Length    Petal.Width
 Min.   :4.300   Min.   :2.000   Min.   :1.000   Min.   :0.100
 1st Qu.:5.100   1st Qu.:2.800   1st Qu.:1.600   1st Qu.:0.300
 Median :5.800   Median :3.000   Median :4.350   Median :1.300
 Mean   :5.843   Mean   :3.057   Mean   :3.758   Mean   :1.199
 3rd Qu.:6.400   3rd Qu.:3.300   3rd Qu.:5.100   3rd Qu.:1.800
 Max.   :7.900   Max.   :4.400   Max.   :6.900   Max.   :2.500
       Species
 setosa    :50
 versicolor:50
 virginica :50
```

The plot graphic is also included in the PDF file; it looks as shown earlier.

As a warning, when I tried to download PDF the first time, it took several minutes for this to work (I am using Windows 10, MikTek).

As expected, the resulting PDF file looks very much like the Latex file in the previous section.

8
Multiuser Jupyter

In this chapter, we will cover the following recipes:

- Why multiuser?
- Providing multiuser with JupyterHub
- Providing multiuser with Docker
- Running your Notebook in Google Cloud Platform
- Running your Notebook in AWS
- Running your Notebook in Azure

Introduction

While Jupyter Notebooks interact with users as the norm, steps must be taken to allow multiple users to interact with a Notebook at the same time. Otherwise, the system overwrites the interactions of one user with those of another. In the following sections, we will explore several options for enabling Jupyter Notebooks as a multiuser platform.

Why multiuser?

The standard Jupyter install is written expecting only one active user at a time. I know, but it's a website. Websites are built expecting lots of users. I agree.

Hence, several groups have come to the rescue to make your Notebook work with a multitude of concurrent users.

How to do it...

We can show an example of the problem if we enter a small (Python 3) Notebook page that interacts with users, as follows:

```
from ipywidgets import interact

def myfunction(x):
 return x

interact(myfunction, x="Hello World")
```

We have a script that takes the string entered and displays it back (defaulting to `Hello World`) with the initial output as shown here:

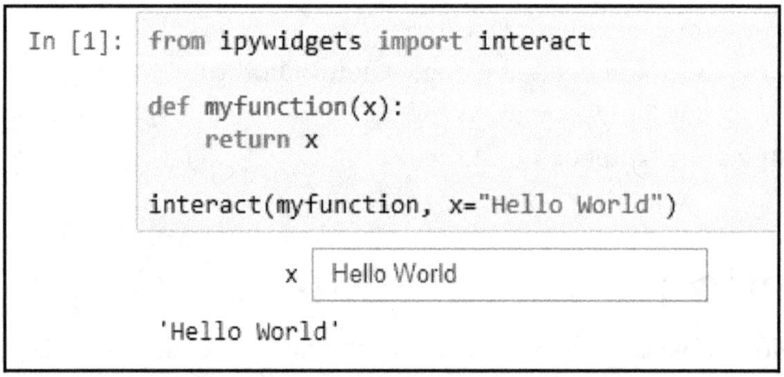

```
In [1]: from ipywidgets import interact

        def myfunction(x):
            return x

        interact(myfunction, x="Hello World")

                    x  Hello World

        'Hello World'
```

And then, as I changed the value entered in the interactive textbox, the display changed accordingly:

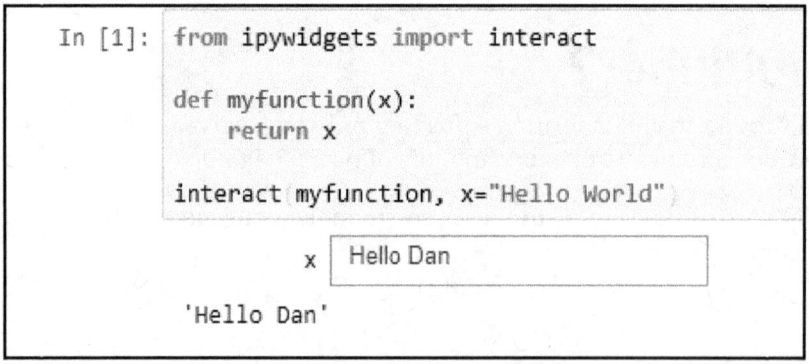

```
In [1]: from ipywidgets import interact

        def myfunction(x):
            return x

        interact(myfunction, x="Hello World")

                    x  Hello Dan

        'Hello Dan'
```

At this point, I have interacted with the Notebook from a browser and it printed `Hello` to me. If I open another browser (or browser window) and direct a user to the Notebook, the new user sees the same display, `Hello Dan`. That is the problem. The new user should see the first screen shown to you before, displaying `Hello World`.

How it works...

The standard Jupyter installation is not multiuser. If you think about this as a program that is running, there is one copy of the variable `x` in the Notebook. When that is changed by one user, all other users see the new value.

We will see different solutions where each user has their own set of values independently of other users running the Notebook.

Providing multiuser with JupyterHub

Once Jupyter Notebooks were shared, it became obvious that the multiuser problem had to be solved. A new version of the Jupyter software was developed called **JupyterHub**. JupyterHub was specifically designed to handle multiple users, giving each user their own set of variables to work with. Actually, the system will give each user a whole new instance of the Jupyter software—a brute force approach, but it works.

When JupyterHub starts, it begins a hub or controlling agent. The hub will start an instance of a listener or proxy for Jupyter requests. When the proxy gets requests for Jupyter, it turns them over the the hub. If the hub decides this is a new user it will generate a new instance of the Jupyter server and attach all further interactions between that user and Jupyter to their own version of the server. Similarly, if the requesting user is already interacting with their own instance of Jupyter, it forwards the request off to their instance of Jupyter.

JupyterHub is not available on Windows.

Getting ready

JupyterHub requires Python 3.4 or better, and we will install JupyterHub. Use `pip` and `npm` to install JupyterHub.

You can check the version of Python you are running by just entering Python on a command line; the prologue will echo out the current version, for example:

```
python --version
Python 3.6.3 :: Anaconda, Inc.
```

If you need to upgrade to a new version, see the directions at `www.python.org` as the directions are OS-specific and Python-version-specific.

JupyterHub is installed with `pip` and `npm` using the following commands:

```
npm install -g configurable-http-proxy
/usr/local/bin/configurable-http-proxy -
/usr/local/lib/node_modules/configurable-http-proxy/bin/configurable-http-
proxy
+ configurable-http-proxy@3.1.1
added 16 packages in 2.382s
```

And the `install` for `jupyterhub` itself is as follows:

```
pip install jupyterhub
Collecting jupyterhub
  Downloading jupyterhub-0.8.1-py3-none-any.whl (3.0MB)
    100% |████████████████████████████████| 3.0MB 486kB/s
Requirement already satisfied: SQLAlchemy=1.1 in
/anaconda3/lib/python3.6/site-packages (from jupyterhub)
......
```

A big part of this install is `oauth`. The `oauth` package is a package used to authenticate users in a system. It presents a login screen and validate their credentials against the operating system.

If you want to run Notebooks locally (on your desktop or laptop), you would need to make sure the Notebook software is up-to-date:

```
pip install --upgrade notebook
Collecting notebook
  Downloading notebook-5.3.1-py2.py3-none-any.whl (8.0MB)
    100% |████████████████████████████████| 8.0MB 180kB/s
Requirement already up-to-date: jinja2 in
/anaconda3/lib/python3.6/site-packages (from notebook)
......
```

This upgrade appears to be a multitude of minor updates to various parts of Jupyter.

Once installed, you should verify by attempting to pull up the help screen for both applications using the help flag (`-h`):

```
jupyterhub -h
Start a multiuser Jupyter Notebook server

Spawns a configurable-http-proxy and multiuser Hub, which authenticates
users
and spawns single-user Notebook servers on behalf of users.

Subcommands
-----------

Subcommands are launched as `jupyterhub cmd [args]`. For information on
using
subcommand 'cmd', do: `jupyterhub cmd -h`.

token
    Generate an API token for a user
upgrade-db
    Upgrade your JupyterHub state database to the current version.

Options
-------

Arguments that take values are actually convenience aliases to full
Configurables, whose aliases are listed on the help line. For more
information
on full configurables, see '--help-all'.

--debug
    set log level to logging.DEBUG (maximize logging output)
--generate-config
    generate default config file
```

```
--no-db
    disable persisting state database to disk
--upgrade-db
    Automatically upgrade the database if needed on startup.
    Only safe if the database has been backed up.
    Only SQLite database files will be backed up automatically.
...
```

From the help output, we see that the configuration options for `jupyterhub` can be passed directly in the command line.

Similarly, for the proxy, we have the complete configuration available from the command line:

```
configurable-http-proxy -h
 Usage: configurable-http-proxy [options]
 Options:
  -V, --version output the version number
 --ip <ip-address Public-facing IP of the proxy
 --port <n (defaults to 8000) Public-facing port of the proxy
 --ssl-key <keyfile SSL key to use, if any
 --ssl-cert <certfile SSL certificate to use, if any
 --ssl-ca <ca-file SSL certificate authority, if any
 --ssl-request-cert Request SSL certs to authenticate clients
...
```

How to do it...

We can now start `jupyterhub` (instead of `jupyter`), with this command:

```
jupyterhub
```

This results in the following display that will appear in the command console window:

```
[I 2018-01-24 03:47:02.175 JupyterHub app:871] Writing cookie_secret to
/Users/ToomeyD/jupyterhub_cookie_secret
[I 2018-01-24 03:47:02.216 alembic.runtime.migration migration:117] Context
impl SQLiteImpl.
[I 2018-01-24 03:47:02.216 alembic.runtime.migration migration:122] Will
assume non-transactional DDL.
[I 2018-01-24 03:47:02.220 alembic.runtime.migration migration:327] Running
stamp_revision - 3ec6993fe20c
[W 2018-01-24 03:47:02.247 JupyterHub app:955] No admin users, admin
interface will be unavailable.
[W 2018-01-24 03:47:02.247 JupyterHub app:956] Add any administrative users
to `c.Authenticator.admin_users` in config.
```

```
[I 2018-01-24 03:47:02.247 JupyterHub app:983] Not using whitelist. Any
authenticated user will be allowed.
[I 2018-01-24 03:47:02.271 JupyterHub app:1528] Hub API listening on
http://127.0.0.1:8081/hub/
[W 2018-01-24 03:47:02.272 JupyterHub proxy:415]
    Generating CONFIGPROXY_AUTH_TOKEN. Restarting the Hub will require
restarting the proxy.
    Set CONFIGPROXY_AUTH_TOKEN env or JupyterHub.proxy_auth_token config to
avoid this message.
[W 2018-01-24 03:47:02.272 JupyterHub proxy:456] Running JupyterHub without
SSL. I hope there is SSL termination happening somewhere else...
[I 2018-01-24 03:47:02.272 JupyterHub proxy:458] Starting proxy @
http://*:8000/
03:47:02.399 - info: [ConfigProxy] Proxying http://*:8000 to (no default)
03:47:02.402 - info: [ConfigProxy] Proxy API at
http://127.0.0.1:8001/api/routes
03:47:02.642 - info: [ConfigProxy] 200 GET /api/routes
[W 2018-01-24 03:47:02.643 JupyterHub proxy:304] Adding missing default
route
[I 2018-01-24 03:47:02.643 JupyterHub proxy:370] Adding default route for
Hub: / = http://127.0.0.1:8081
03:47:02.648 - info: [ConfigProxy] Adding route / - http://127.0.0.1:8081
03:47:02.649 - info: [ConfigProxy] 201 POST /api/routes/
[I 2018-01-24 03:47:02.649 JupyterHub app:1581] JupyterHub is now running
at http://:8000/
```

Notice that the script completed and a window did not open for you in your default browser as it would in the standard Jupyter installation.

If we open a browser at that URL mentioned near the end of the output (`http://127.0.0.1:8001`), we get a login prompt:

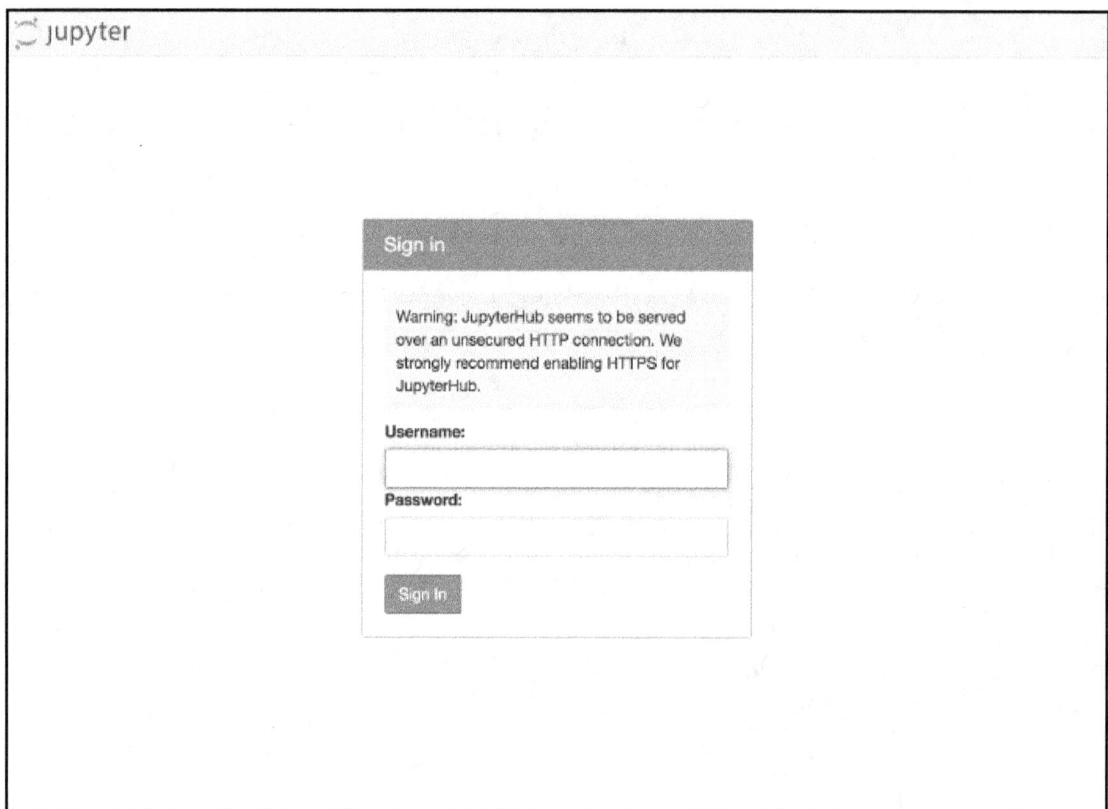

More important is the line of output near the middle, which is also printed on screen in the warning; **Running JupyterHub without SSL**. JupyterHub is specifically built for multiple users logging in and using a single Notebook, so it is complaining that it had expected to have SSL running (to secure user interactions). With the advent of free SSL certificates from vendors, such as lets encrypt, obtaining a certificate for your Notebook is not a major undertaking.

By default, the configuration uses the PEM system, which will hook into the operating system you are running on to pass in credentials (as if they were logging in to the machine) for validation. So, if you log in to JupyterHub with the same credentials you use to log in to your computer, you should see the JupyterHub home page:

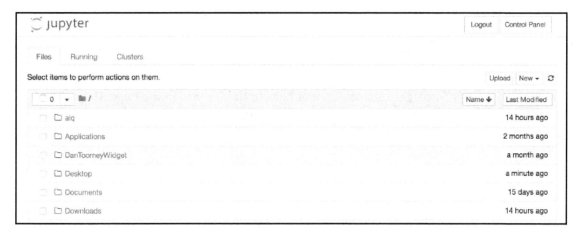

It looks very similar, except that now there are two additional buttons in the top right of the screen:

- **Control Panel**
- **Logout**

Clicking on the **Logout** button logs you out of JupyterHub and redirects you to the login screen shown previously.

Clicking on the **Control Panel** button takes you to a new screen with two options, shown as follows:

- **Stop My Server**
- **My Server**

Clicking on the **Stop My Server** button stops your Jupyter installation and brings you to a page with one button: **My Server** (as shown in the following section).

You might also have noticed the changes that have occurred in the console log of your command line:

```
[I 2018-01-24 20:23:01.181 JupyterHub orm:178] Removing user dtoomey from
proxy
[I 2018-01-24 20:23:01.186 dtoomey notebookapp:1083] Shutting down kernels
[I 2018-01-24 20:23:01.417 JupyterHub base:367] User dtoomey server took
0.236 seconds to stop
[I 2018-01-24 20:23:01.422 JupyterHub log:100] 204 DELETE
/hub/api/users/dtoomey/server (dtoomey@127.0.0.1) 243.06ms
```

Clicking on the **My Server** button brings you back to the Jupyter home page. If you had hit the **Stop My Server** button earlier, then the underlying Jupyter software would be restarted, as you may notice in the console output (which I have shown in the following section of code):

```
I 2018-01-23 20:26:16.356 JupyterHub base:306] User dtoomey server took
1.007 seconds to start
[I 2018-01-23 20:26:16.356 JupyterHub orm:159] Adding user dtoomey to proxy
/user/dtoomey = http://127.0.0.1:50972
[I 2018-01-23 20:26:16.372 dtoomey log:47] 302 GET /user/dtoomey
(127.0.0.1) 0.73ms
[I 2018-01-23 20:26:16.376 JupyterHub log:100] 302 GET /hub/user/dtoomey
(dtoomey@127.0.0.1) 1019.24ms
[I 2018-01-23 20:26:16.413 JupyterHub log:100] 200 GET
/hub/api/authorizations/cookie/jupyter-hub-token-dtoomey/[secret]
(dtoomey@127.0.0.1) 10.75ms
```

The JupyterHub software uses a configuration file to determine how it should work. You can generate a configuration file using JupyterHub, providing default values using this command:

```
jupyterhub --generate-config
Writing default config to: jupyterhub_config.py
```

If you look into your local directory at this point, you will see a couple of files for JupyterHub:

- `jupyterhub_config.py`: The file we just generated
- `jupyterhub_cookie_secret`: Where Jupyter keeps its secret for authentication
- `jupyterhub.sqlite`: Assume Jupyter is using `sqlite` (a relational database) for maintaining its information at runtime

The generated configuration file has close to 500 lines available. The start of the sample file is shown in the following code:

```
# Configuration file for jupyterhub.

#------------------------------------------------------------------------
----
# Application(SingletonConfigurable) configuration
#------------------------------------------------------------------------
----

## This is an application.

## The date format used by logging formatters for %(asctime)s
#c.Application.log_datefmt = '%Y-%m-%d %H:%M:%S'

## The Logging format template
#c.Application.log_format = '[%(name)s]%(highlevel)s %(message)s'

## Set the log level by value or name.
#c.Application.log_level = 30

#------------------------------------------------------------------------
----
# JupyterHub(Application) configuration
#------------------------------------------------------------------------
----
...
```

As you can see, most of the configuration settings are prefixed with a sharp (#), denoting that they are commented out. The setting that is mentioned is the default value that will be applied. If you needed to change one of the settings, you would remove the prefix sharp symbol and change the right-hand side of the equal to sign (=) to your new value. For example, `c.Application.log_format` specifies the layout of log file entries for Jupyter. The default is the name of the component, the level of the message, and a message. Logging format is a well-known software development concept, and it can be changed by removing the sharp/comment mark and adjusting the log format to your desired layout.

By the way, this is a good way to test out changes: make one change, save the file, try out your change, and continue with additional changes. As you progress, if one change does not work as expected, you need just replace the prefix sharp and you are back to a working position.

We will look at several of the configuration options available. It is interesting to note that many of the settings in this file are Python settings, not particular to JupyterHub. The list of items includes the following:

Area	**Description**
JupyterHub	Settings for JupyterHub itself
LoggingConfigurable	Logging information layout
SingletonConfigurable	A configurable that only allows one instance
Application	Date format and logging level
Security	SSL certificate
Spawner	How the hub starts new instances of Jupyter for new users
LocalProcessSpawner	Uses Popen to start local processes as users
Authenticator	The primary API is one method, `authenticate`
PAMAuthenticator	Interaction with Linux to log in
LocalAuthenticator	Checks for local users and can attempt to create them if they don't exist

I made no changes to the configuration file to get my installation up and running.

So, in summary, with JupyterHub we have an installation of Jupyter that will maintain a separate instance of the Jupyter software for each user, and thereby avoid any collision on variable values. The software knows whether to instantiate a new instance of Jupyter or not, since the user logs in to the application and the system maintains a user list.

Providing multiuser with Docker

Docker is another mechanism that can be used to allow multiple users of the same Notebook without collision. Docker is a system that allows you to construct sets of applications into an image that can be run in the Docker container (much like ships at a dock).

Docker runs in most environments. Docker allows many instances of an image to be run in the same machine, but each maintains a separate address space. So, each user of a Docker image has their own instance of the software and their own set of data/variables. Exactly what we are looking for with our Notebook!

Each image is a complete stack of software necessary to run, for example, a web server, web applications, APIs, and so on.
It is not a large leap to think of an image of your Notebook. The image contains Jupyter server code and your Notebook. The result is a completely intact unit that does not share any space with anyone else.

Getting ready

Installing Docker involves downloading the latest version (the `docker.dmg` file for a Mac and the `.exe` install for Windows) and then copying the Docker application into your `Applications` folder. The Docker Quickstart terminal is the go-to application of use by most developers. Docker Quickstart will start Docker on your local machine, allocate an IP address/Port for addressing the Docker applications, and bring you into the Docker terminal. Once QuickStart has completed, and if you have installed your image, you can access your application (in this case, your Jupyter Notebook).

From the Docker terminal, you can load images, remove images, check status, and so on.

If you run Docker Quickstart, you will be brought to the Docker terminal window with a display like the following:

```
bash --login '/Applications/Docker/Docker Quickstart
Terminal.app/Contents/Resources/Scripts/start.sh'
Last login: Tue Aug 30 08:25:11 on ttys000
bos-mpdc7:Applications dtoomey
$ bash --login '/Applications/Docker/Docker Quickstart
Terminal.app/Contents/Resources/Scripts/start.sh'
Starting "default"...

(default) Check network to re-create if needed...
(default) Waiting for an IP...
Machine "default" was started.
Waiting for SSH to be available...
Detecting the provisioner...

Started machines may have new IP addresses. You may need to re-run the
`docker-machine env` command.
Regenerate TLS machine certs? Warning: this is irreversible. (y/n):
```

```
Regenerating TLS certificates
Waiting for SSH to be available...
Detecting the provisioner...
Copying certs to the local machine directory...
Copying certs to the remote machine...
Setting Docker configuration on the remote daemon...
```

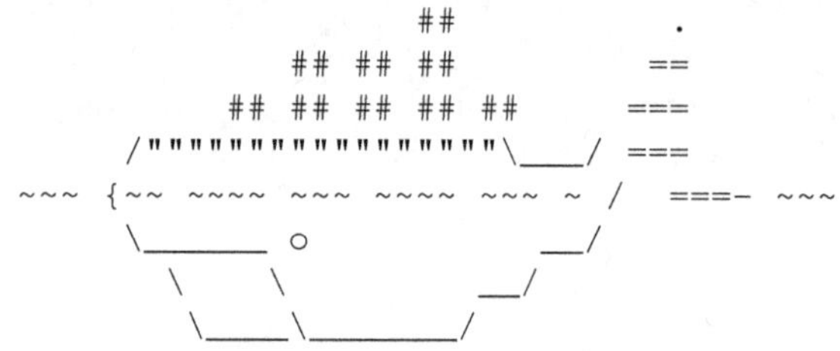

```
docker is configured to use the default machine with IP 192.168.99.100
For help getting started, check out the docs at https://docs.docker.com
```

The graphic near the end of the display is a character representation of a whale, the logo of Docker.

You can see this from the output:

- The Docker machine was started. The Docker machine controls the images that are running in your space.
- If you are using certificates, the certificates are copied into your Docker space.
- Lastly, it tells you the IP address to use when accessing your Docker instances; it should be the IP address of the machine you are using.

How to do it...

Docker knows about images that contain the entire software stack necessary to run an application. We need to build an image with a Notebook and place this in Docker.

We need to download all of the `jupyter-docker` coding necessary. In the Docker terminal window, we run the `docker pull jupyter/all-spark-notebook` command:

```
docker pull jupyter/all-spark-notebook
Using default tag: latest
latest: Pulling from jupyter/all-spark-notebook
8b87079b7a06: Pulling fs layer
872e508604af: Pulling fs layer
8e8d83eda71c: Pull complete
...
```

This is a large download and will take some time. It is downloading and installing all of the possibly necessary components needed to run Jupyter in an image. Remember, each image is completely self-contained, so each image has all of the software needed to run Jupyter.

Once the download is complete, we can start an image for our Notebook using a command like the following:

```
docker run -d -p 8888:8888 -v /disk-directory:/virtual-notebook jupyter/all-spark-notebook
```

The parts of this command are as follows:

- `docker run`: The command to Docker to start executing an image.
- `-d`: Run the image as a server (daemon) that will continue running until manually stopped by the user.
- `-p 8888:8888`: Expose the internal port `8888` to external users with the same port address. Notebooks use port `8888` by default already, so we are saying just expose the same port.
- `-v /disk-directory:/virtual-notebook`: Take the Notebook from the `disk-directory` and expose it as the `virtual-notebook` name.

The last argument is for using the `all-spark-notebook` as the basis for this image.

In my case, I used the following command:

```
docker run -d -p 8888:8888 -v /Users/dtoomey:/dan-notebook jupyter/all-spark-notebook
b59eaf0cae67506e4f475a9861f61c01c5af3556489992104c4ce39343e8eb02
```

The big hex number displayed is the image identifier (automatically generated by the system).

We can make sure that the image is running using the `docker ps -l` command; it lists out the images in our `docker`:

```
docker ps -l
CONTAINER ID IMAGE COMMAND CREATED STATUS PORTS NAMES
b59eaf0cae67 jupyter/all-spark-notebook "tini -- start-notebo" 8 seconds
ago Up 7 seconds 0.0.0.0:8888-8888/tcp modest_bardeen
```

The parts of the display are as follows:

- The first name `b59` is the assigned ID of the container. Each image in `docker` is assigned to a container.
- The image is `jupyter/all-spark-notebook`; it contains all of the software needed to run your notebook.
- The command is telling `docker` to start the image.
- The port access point is as we expected: `8888`.
- Lastly, Docker assigns random names to every running image **modest bardeen** (I'm not sure why they do this).

At this point, we should be able to access the Notebook from an external browser at `http:// 192.168.99.100:8888`. We saw the IP address before when Docker started (`192.168.99.100`), and we are using port `8888` as we specified.

You can see the URL in the top left corner. Here is what we have—a standard empty Notebook:

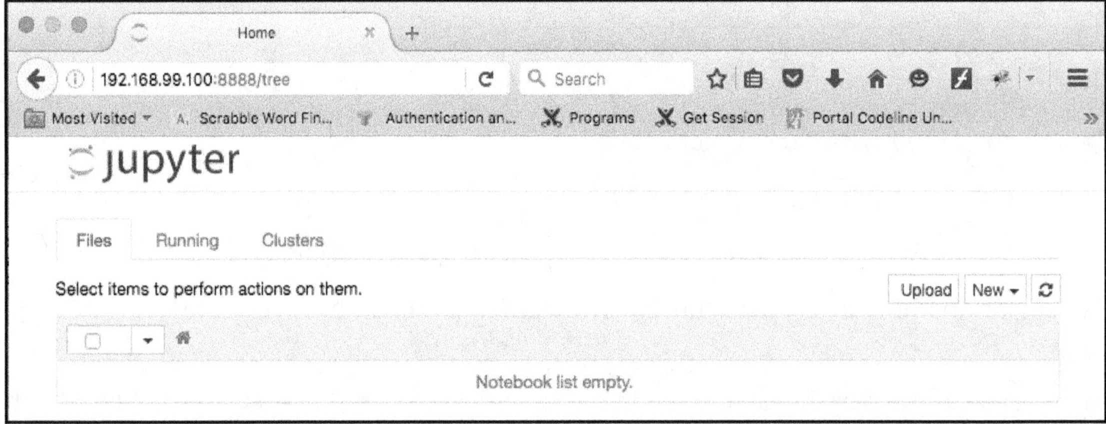

The Docker image used has all of the latest things, so you do not have to do anything special to get updated software or components for your Notebook.

We have installed Docker. We have created an image with our Notebook. We have placed the Docker image into Docker. We have also accessed our Docker Notebook image.

Running your Notebook in Google Cloud Platform

Google Cloud Platform (**GCP**) is a suite of cloud computing services offered by Google. As part of those services, we can run a Jupyter Notebook.

GCP is offered as a subscription and time-usage billing. That means you pay a certain amount per month and you pay for how much you use per month. I think their fees are at par with other hosting arrangements. They have a free trial period that you can try out. Remember to shut down/off any services you start; otherwise the clock will keep ticking and you will get billed.

Getting ready

There are several steps to getting Jupyter installed and running on GCP. Many of these steps are performed using a Linux shell window.

For any of these steps, if you can not locate the item, navigate back to the dashboard (click on the **Google Cloud Platform** button in the upper left corner); at the top center is a search form where you can search for the particular feature.

Set up your GC project

Sign up for a Google cloud account at `http://cloud.google.com`. I think there has always been a free trial available to start you off.

Enable the two services: Cloud Dataproc and Google Compute Engine API.

Install and initialize the Cloud SDK on your local machine. This step is required only if you want programmatic control over your GC installation.

Create a Cloud storage bucket

A Cloud storage bucket is used as a storage area for downloads, uploads, and temporary space.

1. In the Cloud platform console, go to the Cloud Storage browser.
2. Create a bucket. Give it a name, storage class, and location. The class/location value ranges from world-wide, accessed constantly, down to accessed once a year from one user.
3. Click on **Create**.

Create a cluster

On the Cloud Dataproc page, create a cluster.

A cluster means the machines that will be running your project. In this case, we are deploying a Notebook to the Cloud. I selected all of the nominal choices for that use size.

This (and all the other steps of setting up your account) takes a few minutes to get running.

Make note of the external IP address assigned to your VMs (this will be used to access Jupyter), for example, `25.223.122.126`.

Install Jupyter

We are using the Anaconda install script available from `http://continuum.io`. We get the script from their archive and run it in a VM shell (click on the SSH tab to the right of the VM list and one of the choices will be to open a browser shell window). These are all Linux commands.

Download the script

We first need to retrieve the script to install Anaconda. The `wget` command is used to retrieve files over the internet:

```
dan@cluster-jupyter-m:~$ wget
http://repo.continuum.io/archive/Anaconda3-4.0.0-Linux-x86_64.sh
--2018-01-26 02:32:06--
http://repo.continuum.io/archive/Anaconda3-4.0.0-Linux-x86_64.sh
Resolving repo.continuum.io (repo.continuum.io)... 104.16.19.10,
104.16.18.10, 2400:cb00:2048:1::6810:120a, ...
Connecting to repo.continuum.io (repo.continuum.io)|104.16.19.10|:80...
```

```
connected.
HTTP request sent, awaiting response... 200 OK
Length: 417798602 (398M) [application/x-sh]
Saving to: 'Anaconda3-4.0.0-Linux-x86_64.sh'

Anaconda3-4.0.0-Linux-x86_64.sh
100%[=====================================================================]
398.

2018-01-26 02:32:10 (103 MB/s) - 'Anaconda3-4.0.0-Linux-x86_64.sh' saved
[417798602/417798602]
```

Execute the script

We can now run the script that will install Anaconda (and Jupyter) with the following shell command. You need to respond to the script to do the following:

- Press *Enter* to review the license terms
- Approve of the license terms by entering `yes`
- Press *Enter* to confirm the location for the install (I used the default)
- Agree to prepend Anaconda to the program search `PATH`:

```
dan@cluster-jupyter-m:~$ bash Anaconda3-4.0.0-Linux-x86_64.sh

Welcome to Anaconda3 4.0.0 (by Continuum Analytics, Inc.)

In order to continue the installation process, please review the license
agreement.
Please, press ENTER to continue
================
Anaconda License
================

Copyright 2016, Continuum Analytics, ....(continues on for 3 pages or so)

Do you approve the license terms? [yes|no]yes

Anaconda3 will now be installed into this location:
/home/dan/anaconda3

- Press ENTER to confirm the location

[/home/dan/anaconda3]
PREFIX=/home/dan/anaconda3
installing: _cache-0.0-py35_x0 ...
... (continues to install about 100 packages)
```

```
Do you wish the installer to prepend the Anaconda3 install location
to PATH in your /home/dan/.bashrc?
[no]  yes

Prepending PATH=/home/dan/anaconda3/bin to PATH in /home/dan/.bashrc

For this change to become active, you have to open a new terminal.

Thank you for installing Anaconda3!
```

You must close the shell and start another for the install to take affect.

Configure Jupyter

The install does not automatically create a configuration file. You must run the following command to generate a configuration with defaults:

```
dan@cluster-jupyter-m:~$ jupyter notebook --generate-config
Writing default config to: /home/dan/.jupyter/jupyter_notebook_config.py
```

You then use a text editor to add some settings to the file (I used `vi`). Enter the external port number from the preceding VM:

```
c = get_config()
c.NotebookApp.ip = '*'
c.NotebookApp.open_browser = False
c.NotebookApp.port = <port number #8123
```

At this point, our configuration is all set.

How to do it...

We must start Jupyter on GCP by running the command in the VM shell (just as if we were installing locally):

```
jupyter notebook
```

We can add this step to the startup for the VM and it would be available automatically.

We now have Jupyter running on GC. We can use the external IP address configured for the VM and the port we selected to access the Jupyter homepage. I used the default Jupyter port.

Once there, we can upload Notebooks as needed.

Next steps

Never a good time for bad news, but we just installed Jupyter on GC! We actually want to install JupyterHub to allow multiuser. The same steps can be pursued for installing JupyterHub using its install script (as shown in the previous section).

Once installed, the same steps we used right now for configuration would be necessary as well.

There's more...

I don't think this install was particularly gruelling; however, the GC platform was very temperamental:

- Several times, the screen would not paint correctly and I would need to start again at the dashboard
- At other times, the screen would automatically drop me back to the starting place of some process
- A few times, the software just hung and I would go back in the URL to force a repain

Just a warning.

Running your Notebook in AWS

Amazon Web Services (**AWS**) is a secure cloud platform that can be used to deploy web services. In our case, we want to install Jupyter on AWS and deploy our Notebook onto that service.

Getting ready

Signing up for AWS is easy enough at `aws.amazon.com`. Get ready though; the variety of services offered is amazing. For our implementation, we only need a smaller scale server (I selected micro) running Linux (I selected Ubuntu). Unless you are developing a Notebook that would draw a large audience to require a larger machine size, this should suffice.

How to do it...

For AWS, you have to use your own SSH shell; there is no browser SSH connection available (though I was able to do so on GC in a previous section).

There appears to be a delay in deploying on AWS. I am not sure why! There are no hardware changes involved, and all software and allocating another micro instance should be very quick.

Once your VM is running, connect via SSH to your instance. The connection information is presented on the AWS VM dashboard screen. I was running this from Windows and they recommended using Putty, a standard for SSH.

Once on the machine, we install `jupyter-hub`:

- All of this is based on Python. We need to install Python 3.4 or greater.
- Install `npm` (it's the basic tool for updating any piece of Jupyter); we can use this command:

```
sudo apt-get install npm nodejs-legacy
```

- I like using `conda` for Jupyter installs. It pulls in all the features automatically (basically the same steps as before for JupyterHub install):

```
conda install -c conda-forge jupyterhub
```

- Test your installation. If installed, these commands should return the package's help contents:

```
jupyterhub -h
```

How it works...

AWS is a robust hosting service. Providing the hosting for Jupyter is very natural, as all of the system is based on Linux machines.

There's more...

At this point, we have an instance running on AWS. If you leave it there, Amazon will bill you continuously. You need to shut down and terminate your instance. If you used a micro instance, the entirety will be removed from this system on shutdown. This is unfortunate, but the steps to rebuild are very clean.

Running your Notebook in Azure

Azure is another cloud computing service created by Microsoft. Their process is much more interactive, requiring confirmation by phone and the like.

Getting ready

Even though it is Microsoft, one of the choices for resources is Ubuntu with a single CPU. This is probably bigger than the low-end option of the other two services, but is pretty cheap with the expected cost at 50 dollars a month.

How to do it...

Once the machine is allocated, you get a variety of features you can interact with directly:

- The virtual machine
- Disk
- Network card
- Storage
- IP address

All features are directly available as needed

How it works...

If you select the VM, there is a large display of settings for the VM and statistics. If you click on the <_ icon on the upper right, you can open a bash command shell. At this point, you can install `jupyter hub` as described in the earlier section.

There's more...

Like the other services, you need to stop any services you have running. I even went to the step of deleting the `vm` and other resources to be clear that I will not be billed.

9

Interacting with Big Data

In this chapter, we will cover the following recipes:

- Obtaining a word count from a big-text data source
- Obtaining a sorted word count from a big-text source
- Examining big-text log file access
- Computing prime numbers using parallel operations
- Analyzing big-text data
- Analyzing big data history files

Introduction

In this chapter, we cover the methods for accessing big data from Jupyter. Big data is meant to be large data files, often in the many millions of rows. Big data is a topic of discussion in many firms. Most firms have it in one form or another, and they are trying hard to draw some value from all of the data they have stored.

An up-and-coming language for dealing with large datasets is Spark. Spark is an open source toolset specifically made for dealing with large datasets. We can use Spark coding in Jupyter much like the other languages we have seen.

In `Chapter 2`, *Adding an Engine*, we dealt with installing Spark for use in Jupyter. For this chapter, we will be using the Python 3 engine for further work. As a reminder, we start a Notebook using the Python 3 engine and then import the Python-Spark library to invoke Spark functionality.

Most importantly, we will be using Spark to access big data.

Obtaining a word count from a big-text data source

While this is not a big data source, we will show how to get a word count from a text file first. Then we'll find a larger data file to work with.

How to do it...

We can use this script to see the word counts for a file:

```
import pyspark

if not 'sc' in globals():
    sc = pyspark.SparkContext()

text_file = sc.textFile("B09656_09_word_count.ipynb")
counts = text_file.flatMap(lambda line: line.split(" ")) \
    .map(lambda word: (word, 1)) \
    .reduceByKey(lambda a, b: a + b)

for x in counts.collect():
    print(x)
```

When we run this in Jupyter, we see something akin to this display:

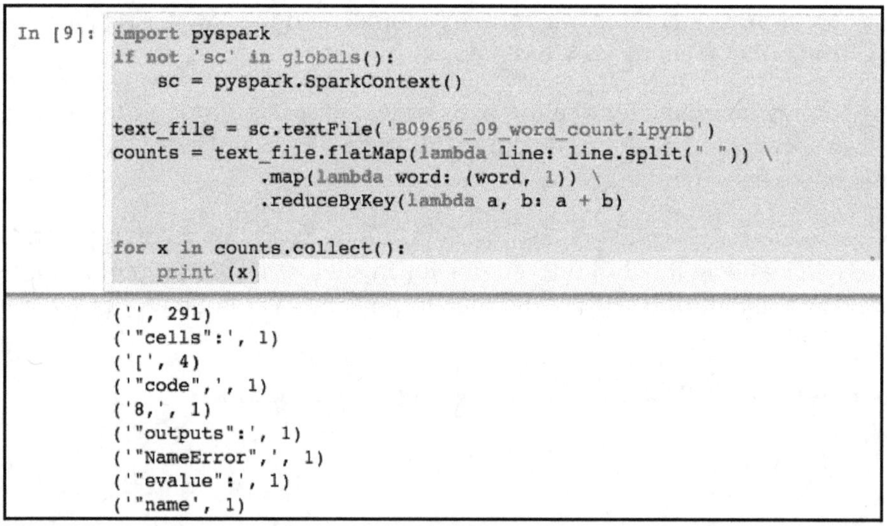

```
In [9]: import pyspark
        if not 'sc' in globals():
            sc = pyspark.SparkContext()

        text_file = sc.textFile('B09656_09_word_count.ipynb')
        counts = text_file.flatMap(lambda line: line.split(" ")) \
                     .map(lambda word: (word, 1)) \
                     .reduceByKey(lambda a, b: a + b)

        for x in counts.collect():
            print (x)

        ('', 291)
        ('"cells":', 1)
        ('[', 4)
        ('"code",', 1)
        ('8,', 1)
        ('"outputs":', 1)
        ('"NameError",', 1)
        ('"evalue":', 1)
        ('"name', 1)
```

The display continues for every individual word that was detected in the source file.

How it works...

We have a standard preamble to the coding. All Spark programs need a context to work with. The context is used to define the number of threads and the like. We are only using the defaults. It's important to note that Spark will automatically utilize underlying multiple CPUs and the like as needed, without specific intervention.

Then we load the text file into memory. This is a standard method available in Spark. If we were accessing a database, we might be able to use parallel operations to read different segments of the primary key to split up the file access.

Once the file is loaded, we split each line into words and use a `lambda` function to tick off each occurrence of a word. The code is truly creating a new record for each word occurrence, like at appears 1, or it appears 2, and so on. The idea is that this process can be split over multiple processors, where each processor generates these low-level information bits. We are not concerned with optimizing this process at all.

Once we have all of these records/words split and recorded, we reduce/summarize the record set according to the word occurrences mentioned.

The `counts` object is called an **Resilient Distributed Dataset** (**RDD**) in Spark. It is resilient as care is taken to persist the dataset. The RDD can be distributed as it can be manipulated by all nodes in the operating cluster. And of course, it is a dataset consisting of a variety of data items.

The last `for` loop runs a `collect()` against the RDD. As mentioned, this RDD could be distributed among many nodes. The `collect()` function pulls in all copies of the RDD at one location. Then we loop through each record.

Obtaining a sorted word count from a big-text source

Now that we have a word count, the more interesting use is to sort them by occurrence to determine the highest usage.

How to do it...

We can slightly modify the previous script to produce a sorted listed as follows:

```
import pyspark

if not 'sc' in globals():
 sc = pyspark.SparkContext()

text_file = sc.textFile("B09656_09_word_count.ipynb")
sorted_counts = text_file.flatMap(lambda line: line.split(" ")) \
 .map(lambda word: (word, 1)) \
 .reduceByKey(lambda a, b: a + b) \
 .sortByKey()

for x in sorted_counts.collect():
 print(x)
```

Producing the output as follows:

```
In [1]: import pyspark
        if not 'sc' in globals():
            sc = pyspark.SparkContext()

        text_file = sc.textFile('B09656_09_word_count.ipynb')
        counts = text_file.flatMap(lambda line: line.split(" ")) \
                     .map(lambda word: (word, 1)) \
                     .reduceByKey(lambda a, b: a + b) \
                     .sortByKey()

        for x in counts.collect():
            print (x)

        ('', 929)
        ('"', 5)
        ('"(\'\',', 1)
        ('"(\'(most\',', 1)
        ('"(\'(word,\',', 1)
        ('"(\'(x)\\"\',', 1)
        ('"(\'+\',', 1)
        ('"(\'.map(lambda\',', 1)
        ('"(\'.reduceByKey(lambda\',', 1)
        ('"(\'1))\',', 1)
```

The list continues for every word found. Notice the descending order of occurrences and the sorting with words of the same occurrence. What Spark uses to determine word breaks does not appear to be too good.

How it works...

The coding is exactly the same as in the previous example, except for the last line, `.sortByKey()`. Our key, by default, is the word count column (as that is what we are operating upon for the `reduce` function). Secondly, Spark automatically sorts the actual words within a word count.

Examining big-text log file access

MonitorWare is a network monitoring solution for Windows machines. It has sample log files that show access to different systems. I downloaded the HTTP log file sample set from `http://www.monitorware.com/en/logsamples/apache.php`. The log file has entries for different HTTP requests made to a server.

The URl downloads the `apache-samples.rar` file. A `.rar` file is a type of compressed format for very large files that would overwhelm the normal `.zip` file format. This example is only 20 KB. You need to extract the log file from the `.rar` file for access in the following coding.

How to do it...

We can use a similar script that loads the file, and then we use additional functions to pull out the records of interest. The coding is:

```
import pyspark

if not 'sc' in globals():
    sc = pyspark.SparkContext()

textFile = sc.textFile("access_log")
print(textFile.count(),"access records")

gets = textFile.filter(lambda line: "GET" in line)
print(gets.count(),"GETs")

posts = textFile.filter(lambda line: "POST" in line)
```

```
print(posts.count(),"POSTs")

other = textFile.subtract(gets).subtract(posts)
print(other.count(),"Other")
for x in other.collect():
    print(x)
```

This produces the output:

```
In [3]: import pyspark
        if not 'sc' in globals():
            sc = pyspark.SparkContext()

        textFile = sc.textFile('access_log')
        print(textFile.count(),"access records")

        gets = textFile.filter(lambda line: "GET" in line)
        print(gets.count(),"GETs")

        posts = textFile.filter(lambda line: "POST" in line)
        print(posts.count(),"POSTs")

        other = textFile.subtract(gets).subtract(posts)
        print(other.count(),"Other")

        for x in other.collect():
            print(x)

        1546 access records
        1525 GETs
        14 POSTs
        7 Other
        h194n2fls308o1033.telia.com - - [09/Mar/2004:13:49:05 -0800] "-" 408 -
        64.246.94.141 - - [10/Mar/2004:16:31:19 -0800] "HEAD /twiki/bin/view/Main/SpamAssassinDeletin
        g HTTP/1.1" 200 0
        206-15-133-154.dialup.ziplink.net - - [11/Mar/2004:16:33:23 -0800] "HEAD /twiki/bin/view/Mai
        n/SpamAssassinDeleting HTTP/1.1" 200 0
```

Interesting that so few other HTTP actions take place beyond `GET` and `POST`! I assume that since this is dated (note that some of the items have a 2004 timestamp), there is no occurrence exhibiting the surge of programming interfaces that are used via HTTP (especially REST API services), which use a variety of HTTP actions.

How it works...

The program reads all the entries for the log file. Once loaded into an RDD textfile, we use standard operations on the RDD to extract our interests. The `filter` function takes a lambda expression and will return true only if the expression is true. In our case, we are looking for lines that have `GET` or `POST` in them. It was not necessary to store these separately. The same results could have been produced completely inline, for example:

```
posts = textFile.filter(lambda line: "POST" in line).count()
```

Computing prime numbers using parallel operations

A good method for determining whether a number is prime or not is Eratosthenes's sieve. For each number, we check whether it fits the bill for a prime (if it meets the criteria for a prime, it will filter through the sieve).

The series of tests are run on every number we check for prime. This is a great usage for parallel operations. Spark has the in-built ability to split up a task among the threads/machines available. The threads are configured through the `SparkContext` (we see that in every example).

In our case, we split up the workload among the available threads, each taking a set of numbers to check, and collect the results later on.

How to do it...

We can use a script like this:

```
import pyspark
if not 'sc' in globals():
    sc = pyspark.SparkContext()

#check if a number is prime
def isprime(n):
    # must be positive
    n = abs(int(n))

    # 2 or more
    if n < 2:
```

```
        return False

    # 2 is the only even prime number
    if n == 2:
        return True
    if not n & 1:
        return False

    # range starts with 3 and only needs to go up the square root of n
    # for all odd numbers
    for x in range(3, int(n**0.5)+1, 2):
        if n % x == 0:
            return False
    return True

nums = sc.parallelize(range(1000000))

# Compute the number of primes in the RDD
print(nums.filter(isprime).count())
```

Producing the output:

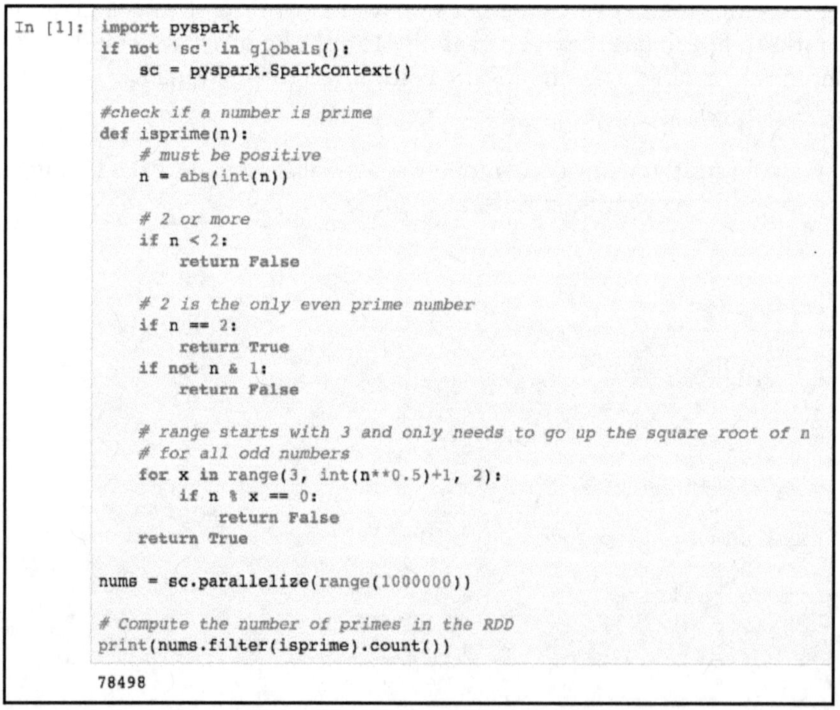

```
In [1]: import pyspark
        if not 'sc' in globals():
            sc = pyspark.SparkContext()

        #check if a number is prime
        def isprime(n):
            # must be positive
            n = abs(int(n))

            # 2 or more
            if n < 2:
                return False

            # 2 is the only even prime number
            if n == 2:
                return True
            if not n & 1:
                return False

            # range starts with 3 and only needs to go up the square root of n
            # for all odd numbers
            for x in range(3, int(n**0.5)+1, 2):
                if n % x == 0:
                    return False
            return True

        nums = sc.parallelize(range(1000000))

        # Compute the number of primes in the RDD
        print(nums.filter(isprime).count())

        78498
```

As you can see in the `isprime` routine, each number is put through a series of tests to determine whether it is prime or not. We use the `isprime` function as a filter for the results (where a `true` result from the function means we account for that number). The result of the script is the number of prime numbers in the first million numbers. If we were to print a logging step into the `isprime` function, we would see it called a million times.

How it works...

Spark will split up the range of values over the available threads/CPUs. Each instance calls upon the `isprime` routine and increments a count if `True`.

The `isprime` routine itself is a clever way to determine whether a number is prime. If you follow along with the steps, you can see that the filtering is easy to understand. The last part of the sieve checks whether the number in question is a square of any other number in the range.

Analyzing big-text data

We can run an analysis on large text streams, such as news, articles, to attempt to glean important themes. Here we are pulling out bigrams—combinations of two words—that appear in sequence throughout the article.

How to do it...

For this example, I am using text from an online article from *Atlantic Monthly* called *The World Might Be Better Off Without College for Everyone* at `https://www.theatlantic.com/magazine/archive/2018/01/whats-college-good-for/546590/`.

I am using this script:

```
import pyspark
if not 'sc' in globals():
 sc = pyspark.SparkContext()

sentences = sc.textFile('B09656_09_article.txt') \
    .glom() \
    .map(lambda x: " ".join(x)) \
    .flatMap(lambda x: x.split("."))
print(sentences.count(),"sentences")
```

```
bigrams = sentences.map(lambda x:x.split()) \
    .flatMap(lambda x: [((x[i],x[i+1]),1) for i in range(0,len(x)-1)])
print(bigrams.count(),"bigrams")

frequent_bigrams = bigrams.reduceByKey(lambda x,y:x+y) \
    .map(lambda x:(x[1],x[0])) \
    .sortByKey(False)
frequent_bigrams.take(10)
```

This produces this output when executed:

```
In [1]: import pyspark
        if not 'sc' in globals():
            sc = pyspark.SparkContext()

        sentences = sc.textFile('B09656_09_article.txt') \
                    .glom() \
                    .map(lambda x: " ".join(x)) \
                    .flatMap(lambda x: x.split("."))
        print(sentences.count(),"sentences")

        bigrams = sentences.map(lambda x:x.split()) \
                    .flatMap(lambda x: [((x[i],x[i+1]),1) for i in range(0,len(x)-1)])
        print(bigrams.count(),"bigrams")

        frequent_bigrams = bigrams.reduceByKey(lambda x,y:x+y) \
                    .map(lambda x:(x[1],x[0])) \
                    .sortByKey(False)
        frequent_bigrams.take(10)

        140 sentences
        2448 bigrams

Out[1]: [(11, ('of', 'the')),
         (8, ('in', 'the')),
         (6, ('to', 'the')),
         (6, ('for', 'the')),
         (6, ('of', 'college')),
         (5, ('more', 'than')),
         (5, ('I�m', 'cynical')),
         (5, ('cynical', 'about')),
         (5, ('The', 'vast')),
         (5, ('vocational', 'education'))]
```

The highest used bigram (excluding base words) is *I'm skeptical of college*. No surprise, if you consider the title of the article! I had expected more sentences for some reason.

How it works...

We use `textFile` to load the file. Once loaded, we use `glom()` to coalesce every pair of words together in the file. We then join them together and produce a map of the entirety (`sentences`).

From `sentences`, we pull out all the `bigrams` (reduced by `flatMap`).

The last step is to pull the highest number of `bigrams` occurring.

Analyzing big data history files

In this example we will be using a larger `.csv` file for analysis. Specifically, it's the CSV file of the daily show guests from `https://raw.githubusercontent.com/fivethirtyeight/data/master/daily-show-guests/daily_show_guests.csv`.

How to do it...

We can use the following script:

```
import pyspark
import csv
import operator
import itertools
import collections
import io

if not 'sc' in globals():
 sc = pyspark.SparkContext()

years = {}
occupations = {}
guests = {}

#The file header contains these column descriptors
#YEAR,GoogleKnowlege_Occupation,Show,Group,Raw_Guest_List

with open('daily_show_guests.csv', newline='') as csvfile:
```

```
    reader = csv.DictReader(csvfile, delimiter=',', quotechar='|')
    try:
        for row in reader:

            #track how many shows occurred in the year
            year = row['YEAR']
            if year in years:
                years[year] = years[year] + 1
            else:
                years[year] = 1

            # what guest occupations were prevalent
            occupation = row['GoogleKnowlege_Occupation']
            if occupation in occupations:
                occupations[occupation] = occupations[occupation] + 1
            else:
                occupations[occupation] = 1

            # what guests were prevalent
            guest = row['Raw_Guest_List']
            if guest in guests:
                guests[guest] = guests[guest] + 1
            else:
                guests[guest] = 1

    except:
        print('got error')

#print out our results
syears = sorted(years.items(), key=operator.itemgetter(1), reverse=True)
soccupations = sorted(occupations.items(), key=operator.itemgetter(1),
reverse=True)
sguests = sorted(guests.items(), key=operator.itemgetter(1), reverse=True)

#top 5 of each category
print(syears[:5])
print(soccupations[:5])
print(sguests[:5])
```

With the results:

```
syears = sorted(years.items(), key=operator.itemgetter(1), reverse=True)
soccupations = sorted(occupations.items(), key=operator.itemgetter(1), reverse=True)
sguests = sorted(guests.items(), key=operator.itemgetter(1), reverse=True)

print(syears[:5])
print(soccupations[:5])
print(sguests[:5])

got error
[('2000', 169), ('1999', 166), ('2001', 16)]
[('actor', 122), ('actress', 73), ('comedian', 19), ('film actress', 7), ('NA', 7)]
[('Bob Dole', 5), ('"Pamela Anderson', 3), ('Adam Sandler', 3), ('Richard Belzer', 3), ('Trac
ey Ullman', 2)]
```

Interesting! About the same number of shows per year. That most of the guests are actors is expected. The most unexpected appearances are by `Bob Dole` and `Pamela Anderson`.

How it works...

The script has a number of features:

- We are using several packages.
- It has the familiar context preamble to our other Spark scripts seen before.
- We start dictionaries for years, occupations, and guests. A dictionary contains a key and a value. For this use, the key will be the raw value from the CSV. The value will be the number of occurrences in the dataset.
- We open the file and start reading line by line using a reader object.
- On each line, we take the values of interest (year, occupation, and name):
    - See whether the value is present in the appropriate dictionary
    - If it is there, increment the value (counter)
    - Otherwise, initialize an entry in the dictionary
- The entire reader block is wrapped by a try/except handler. There is at least one bad character in the file that I cannot locate. This means when we encounter an error, we stop processing the file. There are, however, ways to continue processing the file and ignore the bad records.
- We then sort each of the dictionaries in reverse order of the number of appearances of the item.
- Finally, we display the top five values for each dictionary.

10
Jupyter Security

In this chapter, we will cover the following recipes:

- Security mechanisms built into Jupyter
- Using SSL
- The Jupyter trust model
- Controlling network access
- Additional practices

Introduction

Web security is concerned with assets or information that you have exposed on the internet via a web application.

In this chapter, we investigate the various security mechanisms available for our Jupyter Notebook.

How much risk?

An application would need more security if critical or personal information were used on it; for example, credit cards. At the other end of the spectrum would be a site that is only providing information that is generally known.

In the case of a Jupyter application, you have to make that decision. Is the application or data being exposed of high importance to your company or project? There are many Jupyter applications (or web applications in general) that do not require a high degree of security as the information/algorithms being used are generally known.

Known vulnerabilities

Many web applications are built upon a well-known framework that has been in use for some time. As such, these frameworks have already worked through the known vulnerabilities they expose to their users.

In this case, we have Jupyter, which has been in use for some time. It is built upon a framework (basically Python) that has seen a large number of users address specific vulnerabilities present.

Web attack strategies

Web applications can be attacked using different strategies:

- **Denial of Service** (**DOS**) where a large number of bad requests are made to a web application with the idea of causing a malfunction with the underlying software, thereby denying the service to its real users.
- Web service attacks where different layers of the application are attacked specifically. For example, a web service may have a vulnerability of not correctly handling very large requests, causing overruns in the memory and allowing the attacker to take control of the web application.
- Data theft. Many web applications incorrectly handle data entries, allowing for SQL injections, whereby the attacker can access all stored databases in an application.
- Political motivation. A web application may be attacked by political opponents using any of the tools just mentioned to cripple a web application.

For each of these attack strategies, you will need to evaluate your content, decide the likelihood of an attack, and take measures as prescribed further in this chapter.

Inherent Jupyter security issues

Jupyter provides the ability to run almost any code on a public server. The problem is most apparent in three situations:

- The code executed in a cell is arbitrary. This is completely up to the developer's discretion. Care should be taken to review the exposed coding.
- Shell commands can be run giving direct access to any files on the server or available on the server network.
- A true server shell can be initiated from a Jupyter cell, again giving complete access to the server and network resources.

These issues are remedied by the Jupyter trust policies described in the following points. However, many of them can be overridden by the Notebook author.

Security mechanisms built into Jupyter

Jupyter has a variety of security mechanisms available depending on your needs, which we'll discuss in the following points.

How to do it...

Authentication is the process of proving that the user is as originally presented.

Jupyter can use:

- Token-based authentication
- Password authentication
- No authentication

Current versions of Jupyter use token-based authentication by default. If you enable password protection for your application (the typical username and password that you have seen many times), then token-based authentication is disabled.

Token-based authentication

Token-based authentication is where a token is exchanged for all of a user's requests and it must be present in order for any user request to proceed into your application. For example:

- User K connects to your application
- The response from the application has a built-in token that is generated automatically and passed using web headers in the response
- As the application is running in such a web server, the application knows to place that token in any further requests or responses made
- When the next access to the application is made, the server will check whether the token is present and valid before allowing the request to be processed by the application

Technically, the token can be presented in two different ways:

- An `Authorization` header value, such as `Authorization: asdfasdfasdf....` HTTP headers are normally hidden from view.
- As an added parameter to all requests, such as `http://myserver?token=asdfasdfasdf`.

The additional parameter would be put into the requests automatically by the application.

When a token is `NOT` present, the server will challenge the user for a password to continue.

Password authentication

If token-based authentication does not work in your configuration, you can use password authentication in its place. This is done by setting the `c.NotebookApp.password` field in the `jupyter_notebook_config.json` file associated with your Notebook. You store the hash of your password in this field.

Assuming you have a secret to use for the hash, such as `secret`, you would then generate a hash using this Python script (which can be run in a Notebook!):

```
from notebook.auth import passwd
passwd()
> Enter password:secret
> Verify password:secret
Out[1]: 'sha1:67c9e60bb8b6:923423442ea597d771089e11aed'
```

Take the generated hash and store that in the `config` file parameter, such as:

```
c.NotebookApp.password='sha1:67c9e60bb8b6...'
```

No authentication

If you prefer to have no authentication, then set both authentication fields in the Notebook configuration file to empty, as follows:

```
c.NotebookApp.token = ''
c.NotebookApp.password= ''
```

This would allow anyone to access your Notebook in any manner. Highly `NOT` recommended!

Using SSL

Along the same lines, if you were to determine that the contents of your Notebook are valuable, you may want to use SSL to encrypt all transmissions between your Notebook. At a minimum, then, any authentication information will be encrypted as well and this will prevent hijacking.

How to do it...

A well-known service for providing free SSL certificates is Let's Encrypt (`https://letsencrypt.org/`). Let's take a look at how to create and apply an SSL certificate in the following sections.

Creating an SSL certificate

You can create a certificate using `openssl` with this command:

```
openssl req -x509 -nodes -days 365 -newkey rsa:2048 -keyout mykey.key -out
mycert.pem
```

Where the several options specified are as follows:

- `-x509`: We are using x509 protocol
- `-days 365`: Good for one year
- `-newkey`: We are generating a new key
- `rsa:2048`: Use the 2,048-bit RSA algorithm
- `-keyout`: Location to place the key
- `-out`: Location to place the certificate

Apply the SSL certificate

You can set the SSL certificate to be used by your Notebook with these additional command parameters:

```
jupyter notebook --certfile=mycert.pem --keyfile mykey.key
```

Where `certfile` is the name location of the certificate and `keyfile` is the location of the keystore used.

The Jupyter trust model

Jupyter has specific parts of the application that are trusted or not:

- Untrusted HTML is always sanitized
- Untrusted JavaScript is never executed
- HTML and JavaScript in Markdown cells are never trusted
- Outputs generated by the user are trusted
- Any other HTML or JavaScript (in Markdown cells or output generated by others) is never trusted

Sanitized, untrusted coding is crippled by not allowing access to resources, such as accessing the internet. This can be a problem as many applications would naturally store JavaScript and/or actionable CSS in cells that are not visible to the user but would be crippled as part of the trust model.

Jupyter develops trust for an application by comparing digital signatures. When a Notebook is stored, a digital signature is made using the contents of the Notebook and a secret. The digital signature is stored on a disk accessible by the server. Then, whenever a Notebook is accessed, the signature is regenerated and compared to the stored value, allowing progress only if they match.

How to do it...

We will learn how to override a Jupyter trust model in the following sections.

Trust overrides

A user can override the trust model using two methods:

- Invoking the application specifically trusting the Notebook, for example:

  ```
  jupyter trust http://path/to/noteook
  ```

- Once loaded, invoking the file/trust Notebook method

Collaboration

With the previous trust actions taking place, it would appear to not allow for collaboration between a set of users since each user's key would be different. Jupyter developers allow for trust digital signatures to be a shared location, such as a web server or shared drive mentioned in the configuration file, for example:

```
c.NotebookNotary.data_dir=http://shared
```

Controlling network access

A Jupyter Notebook can control what domains can originate requests to Jupyter and/or what IP addresses can access the Notebook.

By default, notebooks allow for localhost access to a Notebook.

How to do it...

It typically means only you can access your Notebook on your machine. This is enforced with the following parameters in the configuration file:

```
c.NotebookApp.allow_origin = ''
c.NotebookApp.ip = 'localhost'
```

Controlling domain access

You can open access to users on other domains by adjusting the `allow_origin` setting, such as:

```
c.NotebookApp.allow_origin = yourdomain.com'
```

This gives all users in the domain access to your Notebook.

Controlling IP access

Alternatively, and conjunctively, you can control which IP addresses can access your Notebook by setting the `ip` value in the configuration. Using `0.0.0.0` allows all users to access your Notebook like this:

```
c.NotebookApp.ip = '0.0.0.0'
```

Additional practices

There are several miscellaneous steps that can be taken to further the security of your system.

How to do it...

Let us take a look at some of the ways to enhance the security of our system in the following sections.

Server IP address

You can specify the IP address to be used by your Notebook rather than using the default. Many hacking scenarios count on you using default values, such as the port, to quickly acquire targets.

The IP address used by the Notebook can be changed with this configuration command:

```
c.NotebookApp.port = 9732
```

Note that once you determine the port for Jupyter, you need to apply the filter to your firewall so that communication to the Notebook will get through.

URL prefix

The default installation for Jupyter runs at `http://localhost:8888`. While this is convenient for individual use, it can cause problems where other applications may be running at the same port at the server root address. One more tool available is to apply a prefix to the Notebook `url` using a configuration command as follows:

```
c.NotebookApp.base_url = '/ipython/'
```

Here, the Notebook `url` now becomes `http://localhost/ipython:8888`.

No browser

The default configuration for Jupyter will open a browser window on startup. If you are running the Notebook for users across the network or internet, this will not suffice. You can configure Jupyter to not start a browser with this command-line argument:

```
jupyter notebook --no-browser
```

Or, you can use this configuration setting:

```
c.NotebookApp.open_browser = False
```

11
Jupyter Labs

In this chapter, we will cover the following recipes:

- Installing and starting JupyterLab
- JupyterLab display
- JupyterLab menus
- Starting a Notebook
- Starting a console

Introduction

JupyterLab is the next generation of Jupyter. The idea is to try new features of Jupyter in a `lab` environment where some features may be dropped.

There are many familiar and new components available in Jupyter with JupyterLab.

JupyterLab features

JupyterLab has all the features of Jupyter plus the following:

- Drag-and-drop reordering of cells within a Notebook and across Notebooks
- The ability to run native code text files; for example, `sample.r`
- Working interactively between a cell and a kernel to speed up development of notebooks
- Expanding view inline capabilities for other graphical formats
- A large number of extensions to Jupyter for custom graphical interfaces applicable to a Notebook

Installing and starting JupyterLab

This recipe will show you how to install JupyterLab. After installing JupyterLab, we will take a look at how to start it to create your own Jupyter Notebook.

How to do it...

JupyterLab can be installed and started as shown in the following sections:

Installing JupyterLab

You can install JupyterLab using any of the typical install tools. For example, using `conda`, the command would be:

```
conda install -c conda-forge jupyterlab
```

Starting JupyterLab

- Again, this is a familiar invocation, as shown in the following code:

  ```
  jupyter lab
  ```

- This will bring up a command window that has some familiar aspects but with slightly different information than what we have seen with Jupyter:

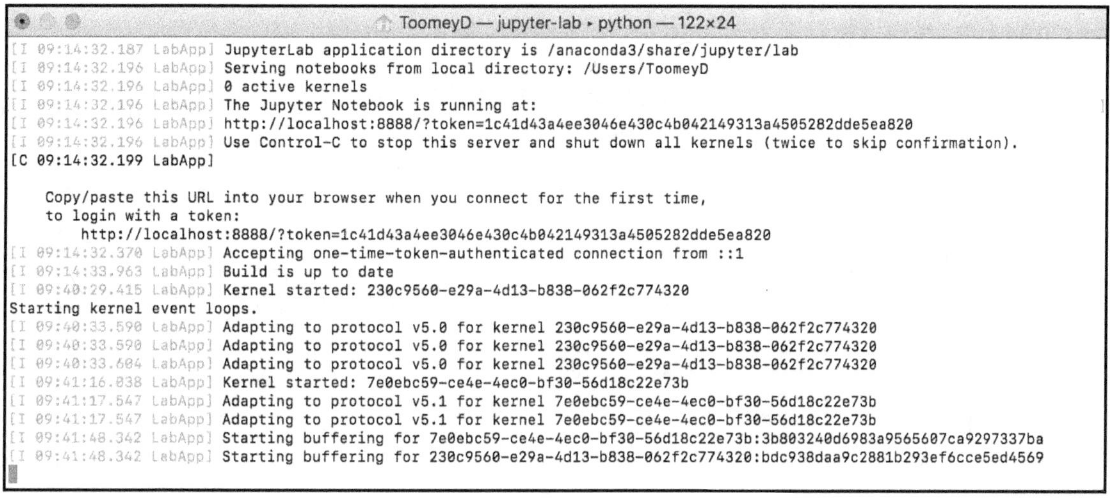

```
ToomeyD — jupyter-lab ▸ python — 122×24
[I 09:14:32.187 LabApp] JupyterLab application directory is /anaconda3/share/jupyter/lab
[I 09:14:32.196 LabApp] Serving notebooks from local directory: /Users/ToomeyD
[I 09:14:32.196 LabApp] 0 active kernels
[I 09:14:32.196 LabApp] The Jupyter Notebook is running at:
[I 09:14:32.196 LabApp] http://localhost:8888/?token=1c41d43a4ee3046e430c4b042149313a4505282dde5ea820
[I 09:14:32.196 LabApp] Use Control-C to stop this server and shut down all kernels (twice to skip confirmation).
[C 09:14:32.199 LabApp]

    Copy/paste this URL into your browser when you connect for the first time,
    to login with a token:
        http://localhost:8888/?token=1c41d43a4ee3046e430c4b042149313a4505282dde5ea820
[I 09:14:32.370 LabApp] Accepting one-time-token-authenticated connection from ::1
[I 09:14:33.963 LabApp] Build is up to date
[I 09:40:29.415 LabApp] Kernel started: 230c9560-e29a-4d13-b838-062f2c774320
Starting kernel event loops.
[I 09:40:33.590 LabApp] Adapting to protocol v5.0 for kernel 230c9560-e29a-4d13-b838-062f2c774320
[I 09:40:33.590 LabApp] Adapting to protocol v5.0 for kernel 230c9560-e29a-4d13-b838-062f2c774320
[I 09:40:33.604 LabApp] Adapting to protocol v5.0 for kernel 230c9560-e29a-4d13-b838-062f2c774320
[I 09:41:16.038 LabApp] Kernel started: 7e0ebc59-ce4e-4ec0-bf30-56d18c22e73b
[I 09:41:17.547 LabApp] Adapting to protocol v5.1 for kernel 7e0ebc59-ce4e-4ec0-bf30-56d18c22e73b
[I 09:41:17.547 LabApp] Adapting to protocol v5.1 for kernel 7e0ebc59-ce4e-4ec0-bf30-56d18c22e73b
[I 09:41:48.342 LabApp] Starting buffering for 7e0ebc59-ce4e-4ec0-bf30-56d18c22e73b:3b803240d6983a9565607ca9297337ba
[I 09:41:48.342 LabApp] Starting buffering for 230c9560-e29a-4d13-b838-062f2c774320:bdc938daa9c2881b293ef6cce5ed4569
```

JupyterLab display

We can see several points of interest in the display:

- We are running JupyterLab versus Jupyter
- The code is installed as part of Anaconda
- New information: 0 active kernels, so we have the idea of multiple kernels running simultaneously
- We see the URL to use if we want to use token authentication (as described in the previous chapter)
- Then, there are several invocation lines as I moved around to different Notebooks in the system

How to do it...

1. Now for something completely different: the JupyterLab display. Once the application starts, we open a new browser window, shown as follows:

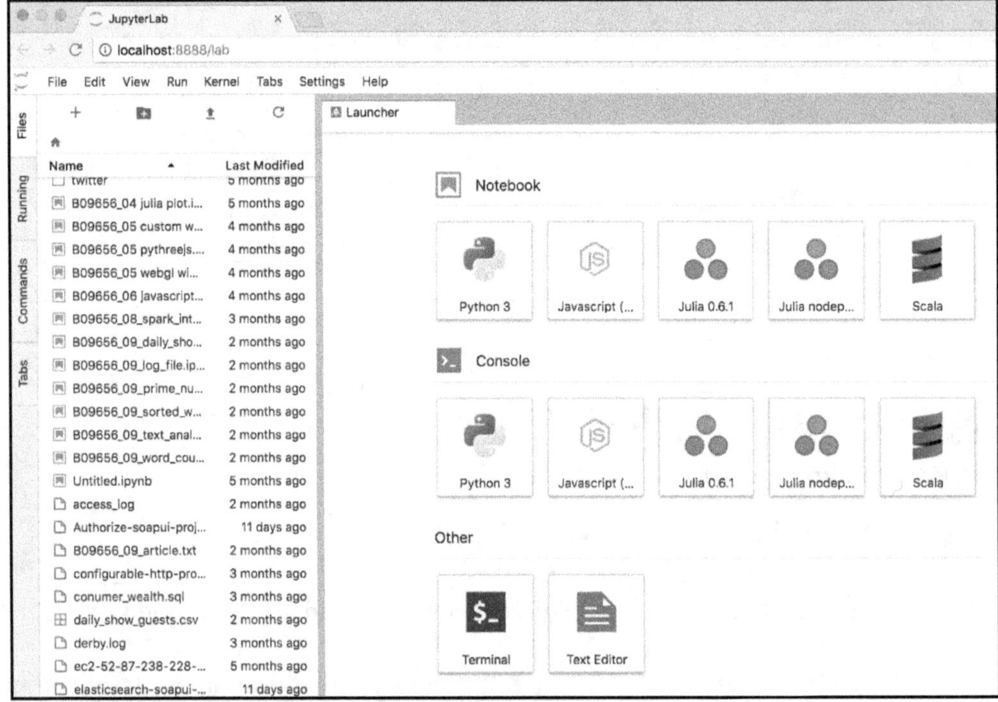

2. The initial display (which is configurable) looks very different to Jupyter, as shown in the preceding screenshot.
3. We have the screen split in two (this can be configured for more).
4. The left panel is the familiar directory display we have seen before. Note that we are seeing filenames rather than the titles applied to the Notebooks.
5. The right panel (also known as **Launcher**) is broken up into three sections:
    - **Notebook**: Engines are available by clicking on a start of a new Notebook with the engine selected.
    - **Console**: Windows that can be started with each of those engines by clicking. This opens a console window starting the language selected.
    - **Other**: Utilities that can be run.

6. Along the left edge, we see actions/adjustments that can be made to the display:
    - **Files**: To display the file list panel
    - **Running**: The display of running engines (as was in Jupyter)
    - **Commands**: Commands available directly
    - **Tabs**: Switch between and change tabs in use in the display

JupyterLab menus

This recipe will walk us through the different menus available once we start our JupyterLab.

How to do it...

1. There are additional menus and menu items available, as shown in the following screenshot:

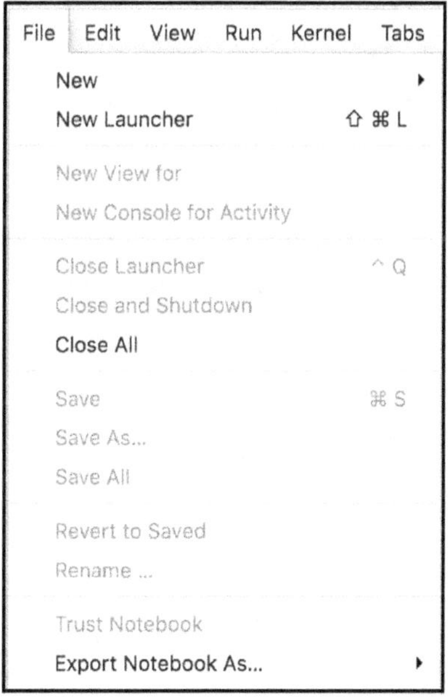

2. The **File** menu includes the following:

    - **New**: This creates a new console, Notebook, text file, or terminal window
    - **New Launcher**: Opens another launcher window
    - **New View**: We can now have different views of the same Notebook—completely configurable
    - **New Console for Activity**: Another console window
    - **Close Launcher**: Closes the launcher
    - **Close and Shutdown**: Menu item versus *Ctrl* + *C* in the console window where Jupyter starts
    - **Close All**: Closes all the programs that are running
    - **Save options**: This option is used to save the Notebook
    - **Revert to Saved**: Notebooks are stored with checkpoints that can be recovered
    - **Rename...**: To rename the Notebook that is running
    - **Trust Notebook**: As mentioned in the previous chapter
    - **Export Notebook As...**: Familiar options to export the Notebook into a variety of formats:
        - HTML
        - LaTeX
        - Markdown
        - PDF
        - ReStructured Text
        - Executable Script, used to store a Notebook script to a direct file
        - Reveal.js Slides, a new format

3. The **Edit** menu includes all the options we have seen: cut, copy, paste, and so on. What is not clear from the menu is being able to copy a cell from one Notebook to another:

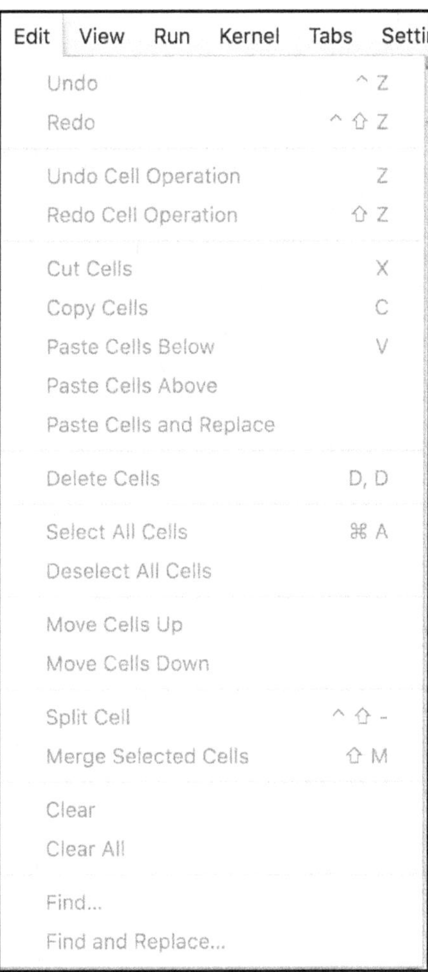

4. The **View** menu allows complete manipulation of the different parts of the display. Of note is the **Presentation Mode** to run in a kind of slide show that we have seen with other tools. Also, the **Single-Document mode** combines the display components into a coherent visual presentation, as shown in the following screenshot:

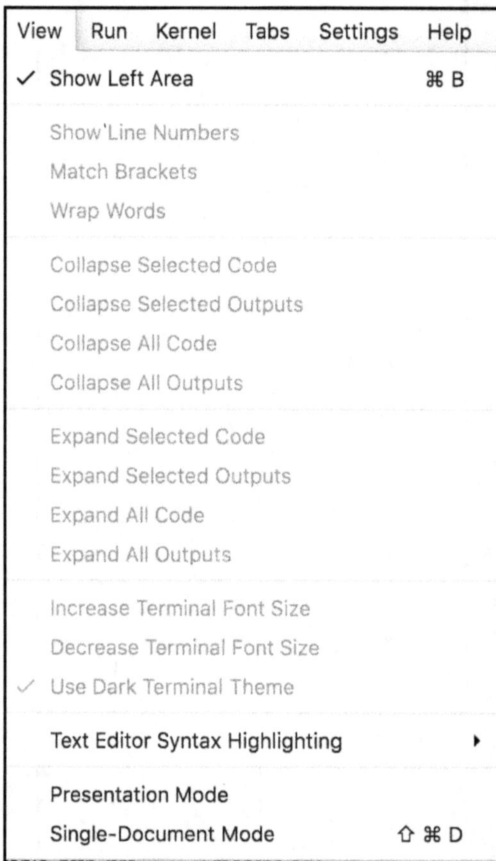

5. The **Run** menu options are all familiar choices from Jupyter:

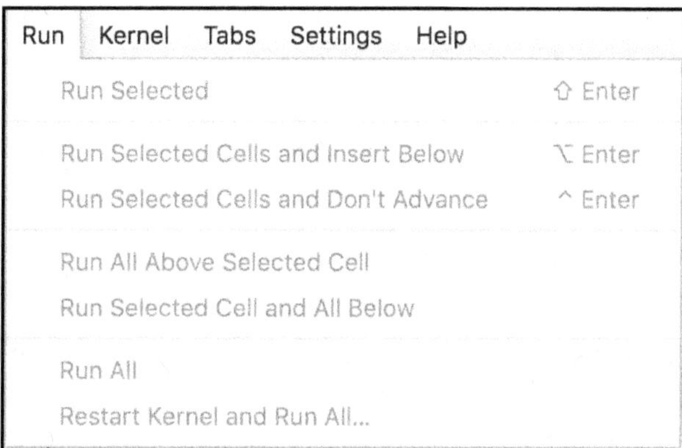

6. The **Kernel** menu options are familiar as well. I think there is more granularity available to each of the kernels restarting:

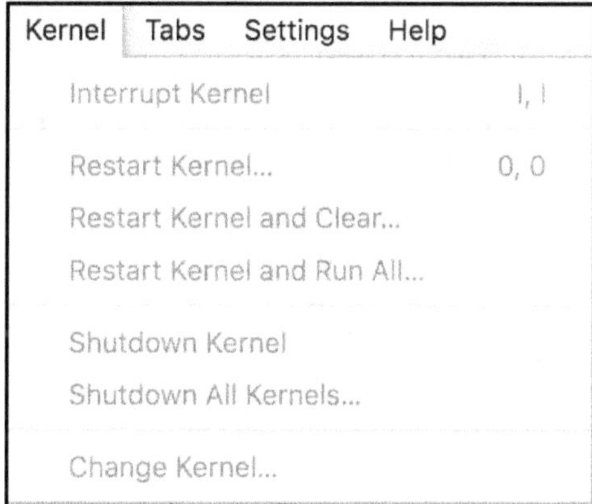

7. The **Tabs** menu is for convenience to move between the tabs. This would be more apparent with a large number of tabs of different sizes in the display:

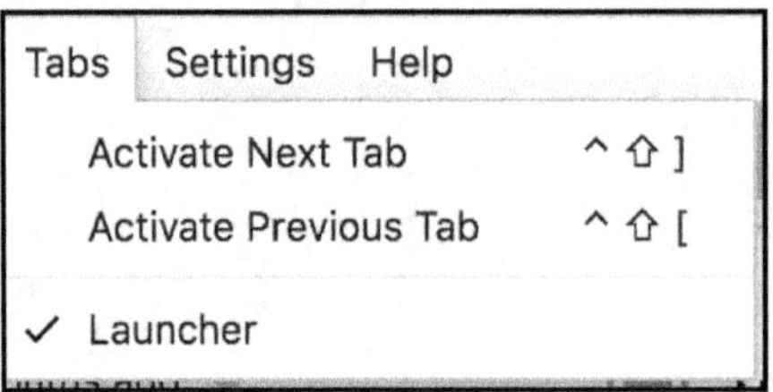

8. The **Settings** menu is nice to have menu options for some of these items that were not directly available in Jupyter. It's interesting to have a theme option where we change the display to different themes as in various other display paradigms, such as Windows or macOS X:

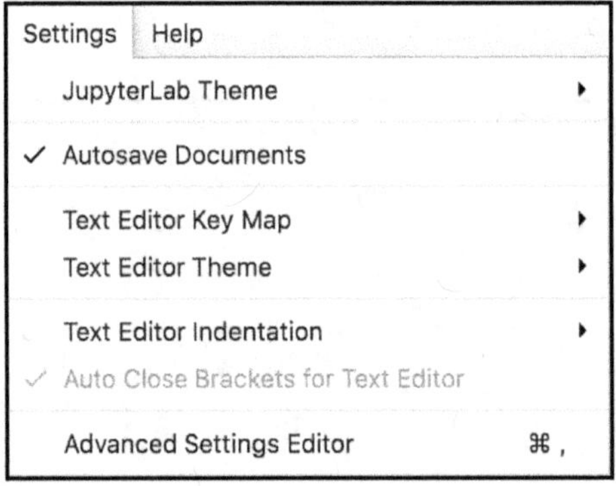

Starting a Notebook

With the help of this recipe, you will learn how to start your own Notebook.

How to do it...

1. Double-clicking on a Notebook in the file display panel will start the Notebook in a new tab in the center portion of the screen, as shown in the following picture:

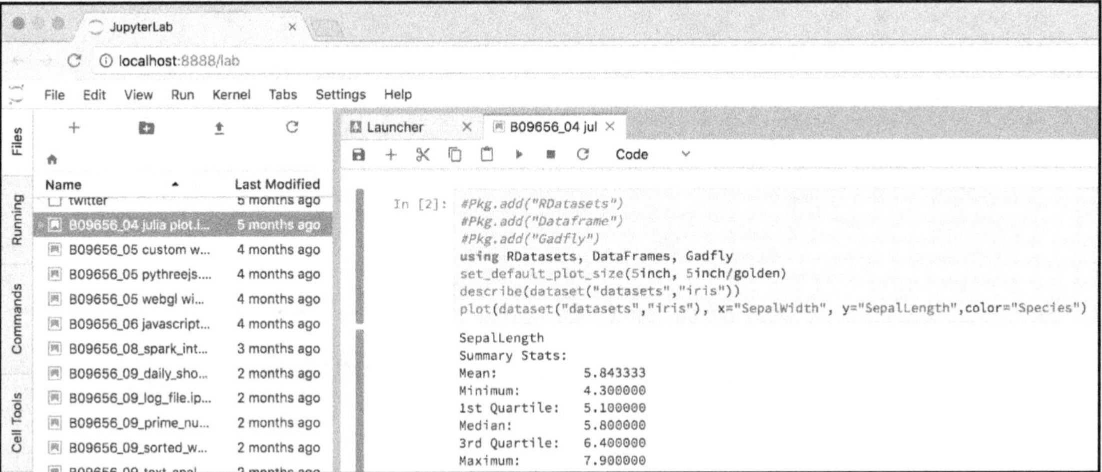

2. Note that the Notebook takes another tab in the center display area. Otherwise, it looks very familiar. There is a vertical bar alongside each cell of the Notebook. To the right of the tab (not shown) is the Notebook engine in use by this Notebook.

Starting a console

With the help of the following ways, you can start the console:

- If we were to select a **New Console** from the **File** menu or from the initial center display, we would see a tab taken up by the corresponding engine. For example, the Python console is shown in the following screenshot:

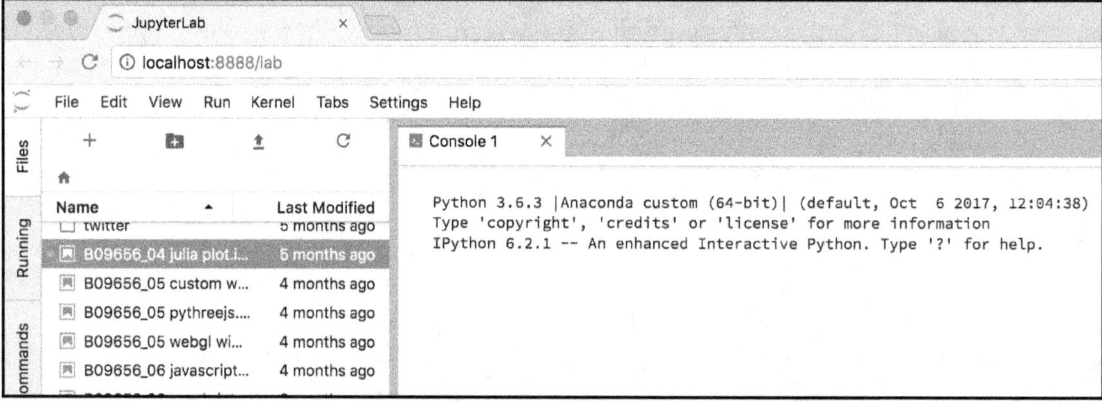

- I think this display change is a great step forward for Jupyter.

Index

www.ingramcontent.com/pod-product-compliance
Lightning Source LLC
LaVergne TN
LVHW081522050326
832903LV00025B/1594

* 9 7 8 1 7 8 8 8 3 9 4 4 0 *